NDTV
Frauds

A classic example of BREAKING Of Law
by Indian Media houses

by
Sree Iyer
PGurus.com

Rare Books

RARE PUBLICATIONS
Chennai

Total Pages : 160
First Published : 2017
ISBN : 978-93-83826-32-2

Published by

Rare Books

RARE PUBLICATIONS

#23,Periyar Road,
T. Nagar,
Chennai – 600 017.
E-Mail : info@rarebooksonweb.com
Website : www.rarebooksonweb.com

Printed in Bharat at
Mani Offset, Chennai

Table of Contents

List Of Tables And Figures

Annexures

Preface

As Managing Editor of PGurus.com, while publishing a series of frauds, tax violations, siphoning of money committed by India's premier TV channel NDTV and its major promoters, an idea struck me to put together an uncomplicated and simple book to educate and disseminate the illegalities committed by this major media organization, which is considered as a holy cow by many people. This book is a classic example of how media organizations misuse, violate laws in connivance with crony capitalists, pliant law firms and politicians to amass personal wealth. This is a narrative of how two Promoters of NDTV along with key top management colluded over the years with government functionaries and politicians to break laws, evade taxes and deceive shareholders of a public listed company. All this obviously through political patronage and "wheeling-and-dealing" as part of the Lutyens club and how they created a biased public discourse for a select elite class.

In the minds of the Indian citizen, there is a space and respect for media. Using the halo of journalism and under the garb of **Freedom of Press**, media owners misuse their position and in the end, degrade the values of journalism. On several occasions media became the tool of false propaganda, blackmailing and illegal money making with the blessing of uncouth politicians and corporate icons with hidden agendas. This ought to be exposed and that is the reason for this book. Once this comes out, I am reasonably sure that NDTV will accuse me of having a hidden agenda. However, the agenda is very clear – to expose the frauds committed by the Promoters of NDTV, which the common man is entitled to know.

Sree Iyer

Managing Editor

PGurus.com

4167 Pinot Gris Way

San Jose, CA 95135.

Chapter 1

Promoters And Companies

India's private sector followed the British till 1947, when India became independent. Thereafter Socialism crept into the society with licenses and permits being required to manufacture even simple things. The License Raj in the name of Socialism ultimately created total corruption. Then in 1991 came the Liberalization policy of P V Narasimha Rao.

When the flood gates opened during the Narasimha Rao regime, a few found that there was a large land grab available and using guile and cunning, and with the right **connections** reaped huge rewards. Throughout India's corporates, you can sense an underlying theme of a Promoter reaping all the rewards and letting his/ her corporate entities (mostly built on public shareholder or bank money) take all the risk. Rarely does one find a Promoter, the individual suing others for defamation; they tend to hide behind their corporate veils, letting the company spend for all expenses and if the verdict goes in their favor, claim victory. This feudal system of **Promoter knows** has also been encouraged by pliant Boards. It is common for Promoters to cheat Banks, Stock

Exchanges and Minority shareholders as they run their companies like a fiefdom.

Add to that a bureaucracy which is only too willing to assist the Promoters in helping them to be in scenarios where the outcome is pre-defined - "Heads I win, Tails you lose". Most of the bending of rules/ regulations happens because the Private Sector gets involved in the drafting of the specifications and thereby tailors them to ensure the outcome they want. In fact, in many such instances, the "powers that be" i.e. our perpetually ruling and non-elected bureaucracy are also appointed by their influence and patronage at key positions in government.

This is one such story.

Chapter 2

Cheating From The Beginning

My earliest memories of New Delhi Television (NDTV) was watching a foreign-returned Psephologist called Prannoy Roy, who used to stay up all night as counting (in those days, it was manual) went on round the clock and updated the eager population of India with trends, results and where the parties were headed. Poll projections were not in vogue yet. What amazed me was that Roy was a constant at the TV network, sometimes for 36 hours at a stretch while the rest of the panelists changed by the hour! As the results caused the fortunes of parties to ebb and flow, when one party surged ahead, its spokesperson turned up and claimed how he/ she saw it all along, only to be replaced by someone else from some other party saying the same things. How did this earnest looking man, with a sly smile ended up presiding over one of the most corrupt media houses in Indian history?

NDTV was built on public money from the very beginning when it started as a private production house and bagged programs from the public broadcaster Doordarshan in the mid-80s. In 1988,

NDTV got a good contract from Doordarshan to produce a famous weekly show called **The World This Week**, which was anchored by the owner Prannoy Roy. As per records, Doordarshan granted ₹2 lakhs ($6000)[1] per episode to NDTV, which was a princely sum in those days. Incidentally the head of Doordarshan at that time was Bhaskar Ghose and his son-in-law journalist Rajdeep Sardesai became the No. 2 in NDTV. The Congress Party was in power then and showed all possible support to NDTV and provided a red carpet welcome to the private media unit to enjoy the national resources of Doordarshan. Every resource and infrastructure of Doordarshan was used for NDTV's growth. In fact, in the early days (1995-1997), it is this tax payer money (Doordarshan contract) that got him personal gains again when he did "sweet" private equity deals (for sale of personal stake belonging to him and his wife) to a few global private equity funds. Thus, he built a business from patronage (government money) and then created value and cashed some of it by selling to private equity investors such as Goldman Sachs, Morgan Stanley, Alliance Capital, Jardine Fleming etc.

Prannoy Roy was appointing sons, daughters, in-laws, nephews and nieces of top officials and politicians in NDTV as journalists. This show of nepotism in journalism changed the style of journalism as access to corridors of power became easy for media houses. Not only bureaucrats, several kith and kin and siblings of top police and military officials too became journalists in NDTV, as and when the organization needed largesse from the system. This unholy recruitment of journalists completely changed the character of India's journalism. In those days the joke in Delhi was that all siblings of the powerful, not-so-good-in-academics can become journalists through NDTV. Still, when you look at the family details of many journalists in NDTV, you can see their links with IAS, IPS, IRS, Military top brass uncles, fathers, and in- laws.

Sandeep Bhushan, who worked with NDTV for almost a decade, told Caravan Magazine[2] that it seemed more than a mere coincidence that the channel should hire so many *"babulog"*—people with bureaucratic connections. Bhushan said that he applied to work with the channel around the year 2000, and gave a "damn good interview," despite which he was rejected. "The next time, I went with clout," he said. Armed with a reference from a bureaucrat, he reapplied for the same post soon after. He was hired.

It is clearly evident that unethical and corrupt practices were the bedrock of Prannoy Roy journalism. After getting the Doordarshan contract through patronage and a quid pro quo, he shrewdly cashed out over ₹23 crores (to his personal account in 1994-95) in a short span of few years (see Table 1 below) by selling shares at astronomical valuations to a foreign investor. Simply put, through political patronage he built a business and cashed out for personal profit.

Table 1. Source: NDTV public issue prospectus filed with SEBI in 2004.

Date of transfer	No. of Equity Shares (Face value of Rs. 10)	Cost per Shares (Rs.)	Price (Rs.)	Nature of payment	No. of Equity Shares (of Face Value of Rs. 4) post splitting
21-Oct-94	48,140	10	675	Cash	120,350
16-May-95	99,070	10	675	Cash	247,675
21-Jul-95	121,625	10	675	Cash	304,063
22-Aug-95	81,481	10	675	Cash	203,702

After inking favorable deals with Doordarshan, many people in 1997 helped NDTV to clinch a magical figure deal with Rupert Murdoch's Star TV[3] during the liberalization period. The Lutyens Delhi's cozy club arm twisted Murdoch into an agreement with Prannoy Roy's NDTV to launch the Star News channel. The message to Murdoch was clear; if you want business in India, you must ally with NDTV. A five-year contract was signed between Star and NDTV for a regal sum of 20 million dollars per year payment to let NDTV run Murdoch's operations in India. The launch of the Star News channel happened at the then Prime Minister I K Gujral's official residence in February 1998.

But during this time NDTV was rapped by the then Minister of Information and Broadcasting (MIB) C M Ibrahim. He was acting on the report of vigilance section of Doordarshan. The Vigilance Section of Doordarshan found that for the past 10 years, NDTV was sucking the blood of Doordarshan like a leech. The vigilance section's report was totally ratified by the Parliament panel also, urging a Central Bureau of Investigation (CBI) probe. The panel found irregularities and financial bungling of over ₹3.52 crores ($985,000) by NDTV in its contracts with the public broadcaster.

In 1998 the CBI registered a First Information Report (FIR) against Prannoy Roy and several officials in MIB and Doordarshan for conniving to siphon public money. The FIR found malpractice of around ₹5 crores ($1.4 million) by Roy and others from Doordarshan's exchequer. Apart from Rajdeep Sardesai's father-in-law Bhaskar Ghose, another top official of Doordarshan that helped Prannoy Roy build his empire was Ratikanta Basu, who later joined Murdoch's Star News. This was a clear case of quid-pro-quo and an apt example of corruption and conspiracy in looting public money.

But luck came Prannoy Roy's way, when his longtime friend Arun Jaitley became the Information and Broadcasting Minister in October 1999 in the Vajpayee Government. All CBI moves to act against NDTV and Prannoy Roy for looting Doordarshan were put in the deep freezer. CBI could not move an inch because Jaitley as MIB totally blocked the actions of the investigating agency and it could not file a charge sheet in the case. And after 14 years, the CBI in 2013, during Sonia Gandhi led UPA regime filed closure report in trial court. The rest is history - The savior Jaitley continued to be present in NDTV screens with his off and on exclusive interviews.

This incident of tackling CBI, using the unholy relations with politicians by NDTV illustrates the kind of grip that NDTV had in influencing action against it by the investigating agencies. Even the Parliamentary Panels which suggested probes of NDTV were ignored. This is the collusion of a corrupt system and media houses, who are supposed to be watchdogs for the common man.

Chapter 3

Beginning Of Hit Jobs And Unethical Journalism

Escaping from CBI cases due to Jaitley's blessings in 1999 gave Roy and his team the courage to do anything and a "license to bend", abet and even be a "go between" in fixing ministerial berths in elected governments (lest we forget the infamous – Radia & Barkha conversations of 2G fame).

The first example was the anti-national reporting by Barkha Dutt during the Kargil war. Due to her closeness with Farooq Abdullah, the then Chief Minister of Jammu and Kashmir and corridors of power in Delhi, Barkha had access to all military installations in Kargil[4] during the war. Her unethical reporting caused harm to the Indian Army in the end. But nothing happened to Barkha or NDTV due to their clout in Delhi's power circles even after alleged anti-national activities in reporting during the war.

By this time NDTV had become part and parcel of Lutyens cozy club of major politicians cutting across party lines. Congress and BJP heavy weights were at the disposal of the TV channel. Moreover Left parties were also silent and complicit on NDTV's illegalities in wielding power as Prannoy Roy's wife Radhika Roy was the sister of CPI (M) Politburo member Brinda Karat (wife of Prakash Karat). Till 2009, CPI (M) General Secretary Prakash Karat and wife Brinda Karat lived with Prannoy Roy and Radhika Roy. Simply, NDTV was basking in the aura of the political, intellectual who's who in the luxurious Lutyens Delhi. Not to forget, by now they had many nephews, nieces, daughters, sons, daughter in laws et al of the powers that be / people at key places on their rolls as journalists or in other positions within NDTV.

After Kargil war reporting, another hit job that was done by NDTV was the venomous and hate mongering reporting of Gujarat riots of 2002[5]. The target was the rising star of BJP, Chief Minister Narendra Modi. This hit job was done at the instance of Delhi politicians in Congress and BJP to finish the political career of young Narendra Modi, who unlike his colleagues never went by media-advised political administration. Angry Hindu mobs rioting in vengeance of the burning of train by Muslims was portrayed as incidents directed by the newly selected Chief Minister of the state by NDTV. Barkha Dutt and Rajdeep Sardesai did everything possible to malign Narendra Modi[6]. Under their leadership, NDTV hounded Modi for 12 years[7]. This was a classic example of Supari Journalism in India. But, an important question that remains a mystery till date is where was Narendra Modi's friend and key ally of NDTV – Arun Jaitley all this while?

Though NDTV is known as a Congress supporting channel, the fact was that even many BJP leaders were supporters of NDTV. Even after casting aspersions on a BJP Chief Minister – Narendra Modi – in 2002, NDTV got its own TV channel running license in 2003, when Atal Behari Vajpayee was the Prime Minister. After eating out more than a $100 million from Star News partnership, in 2003, NDTV flipped the bird to media baron Rupert Murdoch. Knowing NDTV's clout in Delhi, Murdoch did not file any case of cheating against them, as by that time Jaitley had become the Law Minister with hands in several other portfolios.

Another powerful Minister Pramod Mahajan and Deputy Prime Minister L K Advani were also the well-wishers of NDTV, while it was unceremoniously and unethically attacking their colleague Narendra Modi. Many Cabinet Ministers competed in sending or leaking Simple Messaging Service (SMS) about Cabinet Agenda and decisions to Barkha Dutt. Women journalists across the world have had this advantage over their male counterparts. Attraction to the opposite sex is natural, but it is unethical when state secrets are leaked.

The NDA regime led by Vajpayee granted two licenses to run news channels in India – NDTV 24x7 and NDTV India. These English and Hindi news channel licenses were granted to NDTV Group led by Prannoy Roy, when he and the company were facing CBI's FIR for cheating and plundering public broadcaster Doordarshan! While in public the BJP leaders in Delhi expressed solidarity with their young CM of Gujarat, they were enjoying privately NDTV's hit jobs on Narendra Modi, whose career graph was slowly rising due to his able administration in Gujarat. In a dog-eat-dog world of Politics it is not too farfetched to imagine that every Central leader of BJP wanted the collapse of the political career of Modi, whom they doubted as a potential threat to their own political ambitions. After all, at the end of the day there are many senior leaders in Congress and BJP who want to die after becoming either the Prime Minister or the President of India.

Every rule was bent for NDTV when they started their own two channels in English and Hindi. The investors were pouring in as MIB and Finance Ministry shut their eyes on imposing the strict rules of foreign money investment in news channels in India. NDTV even acquired a Helicopter[2] to go for coverage, despite objections from Civil Aviation Ministry. Several State Chief Ministers from all parties were pleased to help NDTV in setting up plush offices as news bureaus. The sons, daughters, nephews and nieces of powerful people in state administrations landed as journalists in NDTV. All rules were flouted during the Vajpayee regime for NDTV, though it was mercilessly attacking with wrong, malicious reports against party's Gujarat Chief Minister Narendra Modi.

After the Sonia Gandhi led UPA came to power with the support of Left parties in 2004, NDTV's golden days started. NDTV became a go between with Congress leadership and its other partners. Money started pumping into NDTV from all tax havens in the World, violating all norms of Finance Ministry during P Chidambaram's tenure. Padma Shri awards were granted to Barkha Dutt and Rajdeep Sardesai for their "meritorious service". NDTV can be thought of as one of the originators of paid journalism, especially during the 10 year long Congress regime and was at last exposed in the Niira Radia tapes.

Several illegalities of tax evasion were done by NDTV during the Congress regime. UPA's Finance Ministers P Chidambaram and Pranab Mukherjee were competing to dole out gifts to NDTV. When Pranab

Mukherjee became the President of India, he went to the extent of allowing NDTV to conduct its 25th anniversary in Rashtrapati Bhavan! This was the first instance in Independent India, when the Rashtrapati Bhavan was thrown open for a private function, which was blessed by Who's Who in Government, Politics, Intelligentsia and Business tycoons in 2013.

Income Tax (IT) Commissioner S K Srivastava's attempts to act against NDTV were curtailed by the then Finance Minister Chidambaram. The officer was hounded by the system which made him collapse physically and mentally for a while. The illegalities of tax violations and money siphoning by NDTV and its major shareholder Prannoy Roy will be discussed in detail with evidence in the coming chapters.

NDTV was getting one investor after the other during the UPA regime. Mukesh Ambani and Naveen Jindal's father in law's Oswal Group were funding NDTV. Niira Radia tapes tell us that she brought Mukesh Ambani to NDTV. One must remember that these were the days of 2G, Coal, Krishna Godavari (KG) Basin scams[8] under the leadership of Sonia Gandhi led Government. NDTV was accepting money from all the culprits in the scams. Now it is found that NDTV even had a money trail of $50 million from Malaysia's Maxis Group which was illegally allowed to take over Aircel mobile phone operator by Chidambaram in 2006.

During the UPA regime of 10 years, the only major news breaks aired by NDTV were the hit jobs against Narendra Modi. The Congress regime would plant all hit jobs against Modi either in NDTV or in Tarun Tejpal's Tehelka. And what happened to such so called news breaks against Modi? Be it Sohrabuddin Sheikh or terrorist Ishrat Jehan encounter or the Best Bakery case or any other Gujarat riot cases, nothing illegal was ever found. Teesta Setalvad and police officer Sanjeev Bhatt's depositions etc were published by NDTV with much fanfare and parroted by Congress and Left liberals but in the end both fizzled out.

Of course, it is relevant to mention some instances of proximity of key NDTV personnel to the UPA dispensation – Sonia Singh is the wife of R P N Singh (who was the then Home Minister of State) and another lady – Nidhi Razdan has been talked about as being close to Omar Abdullah (the then ally of Congress and Chief Minister of Jammu and Kashmir). Besides many other top personnel such as NDTV Group CEO - K V L Narayan Rao (son of the former Chief of Army Staff – Gen K V Krishna Rao) etc., was in the IRS (Income Tax Dept). Now the latest, Sarah Jacob (who hosts the famous We the People talk show post Barkha's exit from NDTV) is the daughter in law of Montek Singh Ahluwalia. One can clearly accept and fathom how the "privileged access party continued" for so many years.

But media is not the World. Now Modi is the Prime Minister of India with a decisive majority. This shows that people have seen through the waves of hit jobs by NDTV. Will the NDTV journalists one day sit and think about the sins they committed for more than a decade against Narendra Modi?

Chapter 4

Muzzling The Whistleblower Income Tax Officer

While NDTV was all out enjoying during the UPA tenure, its misfortunes started when an honest Income Tax Official S K Srivastava, IRS detected frauds in accounting in early 2006. He found that his junior Income Tax official Shumana Sen IRS was conniving with NDTV in fudging the accounts[9]. Shumana Sen was the Assessing Officer of NDTV's Income Tax circle and her husband Abhisar Sharma was a journalist cum news presenter of NDTV. This itself is a serious Income Tax violation in that Shumana Sen had never declared to the department that her husband was a staffer of the company on which she was assessing tax.

Srivastava first found the fraud committed by Shumana Sen by illegally granting a reimbursement of ₹1.41 crores ($325,000)[10] to NDTV. He then found a series of favors she received from NDTV for hushing up the fudging in accounts by the TV channel, which employed her husband at an exorbitant salary of more than 15 lakhs per annum in 2005, while most of the prominent journalists were getting around half of that. Many favors were granted to Shumana Sen including foreign vacations. Srivastava also found that another lady officer Ashima Neb IRS was also part of this corrupt racket.

Income Tax Commissioner Srivastava did a deep dive into NDTV's Income Tax Returns. He found several illegalities and money routing (laundering) through a series of shell companies floated abroad. He found similarities in NDTV schemes that mirrored those of Chidambaram in many of these money trails. Srivastava then went on record and started reporting to higher-ups on his findings. And that is when problems started for him.

NDTV's mentor Finance Minister Chidambaram became furious and Srivastava started facing his wrath. Many false cases including sexual harassment were slapped on Srivastava by the department. He was suspended from service. All attempts were made to ruin him financially and mentally. He started meeting many public-spirited persons and media persons and all kept quiet initially. Nobody dared to act on the revelations of an Income Tax Commissioner, fearing the clout of NDTV and Chidambaram. He was hounded like a mad dog by the venal interests.

These atrocities against the honest officer came to public domain only after Chidambaram left Finance

Ministry in December 2008 to become the Home Minister. Pranab Mukherjee took a lenient view by stopping the illegal orders issued against Srivastava. Meanwhile, Srivastava got the support of noted journalist and financial analyst S Gurumurthy, veteran lawyer Ram Jethmalani and noted activist Madhu Kishwar. if these three had not turned-up, the evil forces would have finished off Srivastava, who was by then in considerable mental distress.

The country was witnessing an anti-corruption wave after the exposé of 2G Scam. Srivastava also started filing complaints in several forums. Due to his mental condition at that time, he was fined by some courts due to the harsh language used in his petitions. Meanwhile Chidambaram was back in the Finance Ministry in mid 2012 and started unleashing all dirty tricks against Srivastava by stalling to re-instate him. In every forum, the government lost its service cases against Srivastava and Chidambaram was busy with his machinations from the back end to prevent him from getting back into service.

But time has proved that most of Srivastava's findings were correct. His doubts on the money laundering through shell companies floated abroad are now proved right. All the allegations launched against Srivastava were found manipulated and wrong. The

NDA Government led by Narendra Modi re-instated him back in service.

The Income Tax investigation found that Journalist Abhisar Sharma's Gross Unlawful income was ₹4.08 crores ($610,000). His wife, IRS Officer Shumana Sen's Gross Unlawful income was ₹7 crores ($1.046 million)[11] and her partner in crime IRS Officer Ashima Neb's Gross Unlawful income was ₹2.93 crores ($438,000) . Based upon Income Tax findings, CBI also registered preliminary enquiry against these people.

(Refer Annex I)

Chapter 5

Minority Shareholder Revolts

NDTV started facing the music of law when in 2013, its minority shareholders Sanjay Dutt and Sanjay Jain of Quantum Securities Private Limited, approached Securities and Exchange Board of India (SEBI) with a series of complaints. These complaints exposed a long list of violations of Promoters and key management of NDTV by fudging accounts, money laundering by floating shell companies across the world. These complaints became the real turning point, forcing Income Tax and Enforcement Directorate to act when the NDA Government came to power.

But the Finance Minister Arun Jaitley was doing his best to put hurdles in every action of the Income Tax, SEBI and Enforcement Directorate. Now NDTV's lootings are on the radar of CBI and Delhi Police's Economic Offences Wing (EOW) too and it is rumored that a Preliminary Enquiry (PE) or a Regular Case (RC) is likely to be registered soon.

Meanwhile, Prannoy Roy tried every trick in the book to discredit Sanjay Dutt and Sanjay Jain. Prannoy even filed a false case of extortion against the minority shareholders! However post a proper investigation, the honest officers of Delhi Police rejected to file the case (an FIR), after finding that all allegations made were baseless/ fabricated. Prannoy Roy and gang had called the minority shareholders for compromise talks, led them along by spinning stories and loose talk at NDTV office and secretly recorded the conversations and gave to police selected videos and audios of some of the heated conversations related to money settlement. Delhi Police found the fraud and rejected the case and specifically mentioned in the reports that discussions were for legitimate dues to Sanjay Dutt and Sanjay Jain. Though many corrupt politicians put pressure on Delhi Police in 2016 to register a case against the minority shareholders, the Police resisted undue pressure and remained firm on the legitimate investigations. Why would two persons who (on invitation) went to NDTV office and carry out extortion/ threaten them? The NDTV management was trying to trap them in a **false case** through a **fake sting** operation.

A little background on Sanjay Dutt and associates (Quantum Securities and other companies linked to him is relevant here). Sanjay Dutt has known Prannoy Roy and Vikram Chandra for over 3 decades as a close family friend and of course, Vikram Chandra was in the same school as Sanjay Dutt in Dehradun in 1980's. In fact, it was in 2006 that Vikram Chandra approached Sanjay Dutt (a successful equity broker and qualified chartered accountant) to assist NDTV in raising funds overseas and working along with their team as consultants. When Sanjay Dutt along with his colleague Sanjay Jain took up the consulting assignment with NDTV, Sanjay Dutt and his associate companies/ family held substantial shareholding in NDTV. The shareholding at that point of time was close to 2% and then it went up to 3% or say around 17 lakh shares. Besides this pecuniary interest, Sanjay Dutt and Sanjay Jain (also a chartered accountant with substantial experience in financial markets) were also offered incentive shares in the foreign subsidiary of NDTV (NDTV Networks Plc) as stock options/ milestone based incentives. This incentive was around ₹40-45 crores (clearly documented in the Delhi Police investigation) based on the fact that they helped in raising close to 250-270 million USD for NDTV in a short span of 18-24 months from June 2006 to May 2008.

It is believed that the main reason of the fall out between Dutt and Jain with NDTV was the fact that Prannoy Roy did not honor his commitment and in fact back stabbed them by throwing them out and accusing them of causing loss to NDTV (as stated in the Police Complaint also). Further, it is relevant here that when Sanjay Jain and Dutt quit in May – June 2008, the shareholding of Dutt associates (in NDTV) was worth over ₹75-80 crores (close to 1.7 million shares at 450/- a piece). One learns that **contrary to what Prannoy Roy did** to Sanjay Dutt and Sanjay Jain, they (Dutt and Jain) **still did not tender their shares** in the open offer (that was ongoing when they quit in June-July 2008). In fact, they **continued to believe in NDTV** and did not want to let down Prannoy by saddling him with their shares as every share tendered in the open offer (made by Prannoy and Radhika) were accepted at the then offer price that would have led to substantial profits to Dutt and associates. Post the fallout, they sold nearly all their shares at substantial loss as the price from a high of ₹500 odd fell to ₹26 in 2010-2011.

Table 2 below shows the ownership details of the Roys and how they committed fraud.

Table 2. Fraudulent trades/shares sales & purchase to hoodwink shareholders, tax authorities, SEBI and MIB

Books / Balance Sheet of RRPR Holding Pvt. Ltd.							
Date	Particulars from RRPR Holding Pvt. Ltd Books/Filings	No. of Shares	Cost per Shares (Rs.)	Total cost of acquisition Rs.	Cumulative Balance of Shares held	% age of stake in NDTV	Comments/ Explanations/ Notes
3-Mar-08	Purchased in open offer	97,95,434	438/ 98	429,99,99,618	97,95,434	15.64	Financed with India Bulls Loan with a misstatement in the Offer Document that Promoters had the resources in Dec 2007
14-Jul-08	Sold	(38,03,728)	446	1,69,73,38,496	59,91,706	9.55	As agreed in a covert understanding / binding agreement with Goldman Sachs on 7.3.2008 in violation of SEBI Disclosure and Takeover Regulations
8-Aug-08	Sold	(12,49,985)	409	51,07,03,247	47,41,721	7.56	- Same as above - In addition, a covert agreement to appoint a Goldman nominee on the Board of NDTV.
3-Aug-09	Purchased from Mrs. Radhika Roy	57,81,841	4	2,31,27,364	1,05,23,562	16.78	Once again part of an illegal & covert agreement (dated 21.07.2009) to sell 26% stake in NDTV to VCPL. These were done to facilitate VCPL to get 26% in RRPR Holdings and transfer of ownership of RRPR to VCPL
3-Aug-09	Purchased from Dr. Prannoy Roy	57,81,842	4	2,31,27,368	1,63,05,404	26	- Same as above - VCPL paid Rs. 350 crores for a 26% stake in NDTV at a valuation of 1346 crores vs. market price of 795 crores.
8-Mar-10	Shares sold to Mrs. Radhika Roy	(34,78,925)	4	1,39,15,700	1,28,26,479	20.45	All the March 8th, 2010 trades were done to pass illegal gains (as established by Income Tax Dept) to Radhika Roy and Prannoy Roy
8-Mar-10	Shares sold to Dr. Prannoy Roy	(34,78,925)	4	1,39,15,700	93,47,554	14.5	- same as above -
8 Mar 2010	Purchased from joint A/c	48,36,850	140	67,71,59,000	1,41,84,404	22	These same day trades of buying and selling with a price
8-Mar-10	Purchased from Mrs. Radhika Roy	23,14,762	140	32,40,66,680	1,64,99,166	25.6	differential of over 98% from market price. All done only to
8-Mar-10	Purchased from Dr. Prannoy Roy	23,14,762	140	32,40,66,680	1,88,13,928	29.19	generate illegal (hawala) gains for Radhika Roy and Prannoy Roy. This enabled them to siphon VCPL money into personal accounts.

31

Even if one were to estimate conservatively, on July 21 2009, (shown in the table above as on **Aug 3, 2009** giving time for the paperwork to be completed) the shareholders of NDTV were cheated by ₹108 crores or ₹86 per share when the market price itself on that day was ₹127. Another glaring fact – look at the trades that happened on March 8, 2010. The share price was either ₹4 a share or ₹140! The Roys made a killing on that day!!!

As of May 2016, the shareholding pattern, per public records (Bombay Stock Exchange filings) is shown in the Figure 1 below:

Figure 1. NDTV Shareholding pattern (45K is 45,000)

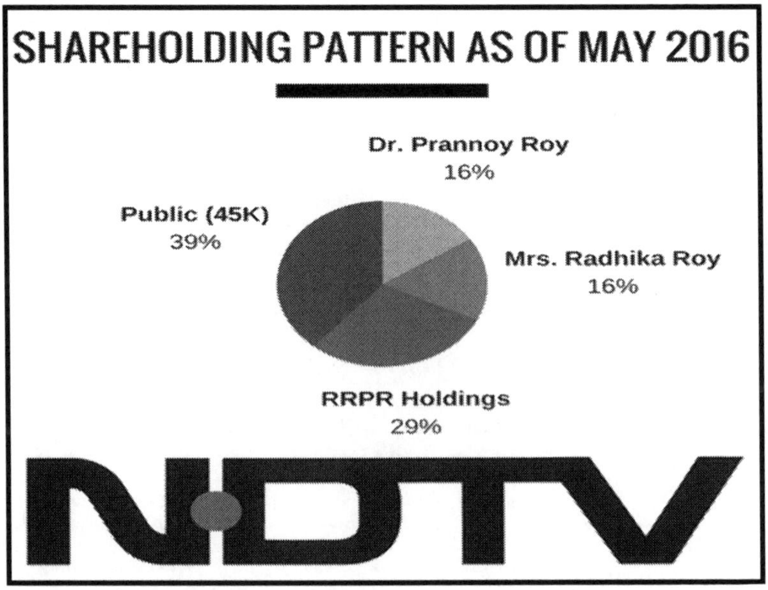

Ever since 2012-2013, SEBI did not take any action on

the wrongdoings by Prannoy Roy and Radhika Roy that caused substantial personal gains to them. In fact, SEBI kept silent on the minority shareholder's series of complaints and was forced to act only after the shareholder approached Delhi High Court. It is believed that the current SEBI Chairman along with Finance Ministry's senior officials were forcing SEBI to keep silent and it was only the Delhi High Court that ordered Enforcement Directorate and Income Tax Department to file probe status of the minority shareholder, Quantum Securities Pvt. Ltd's complaints on January 12, 2017. Not only on the complaints filed by the petitioner, Justice Sanjeev Sachdeva also ordered the agencies to file probe status of all complaints against NDTV for the past six years. The other complainants were BJP leader Subramanian Swamy, journalist and financial analyst S Gurumurthy, former Finance Minister Yashwant Sinha, former Chief Justice of India R C Lahoti, former Punjab DGP K P S Gill and whistleblower Income Tax Commissioner S K Srivastava. The larger question is why ED, SEBI and IT sat on these complaints filed by prominent persons from 2010? The answer is simple: SEBI, ED and IT are under Finance Ministry and all Ministers – P Chidambaram, Pranab Mukherjee and Arun Jaitley - from 2004 were protecting NDTV.

The details of complaints filed by the minority shareholders Sanjay Dutt and Sanjay Jain led Quantum Securities Private Limited is shocking. One of the frauds committed by Prannoy Roy was the creation of a shell company called RRPR Holdings Private Limited and grabbing Stock Exchange listed company NDTV's major controlling shares. What is RRPR Holdings? It is Radhika Roy Prannoy Roy Holdings. Husband and wife each have 50 percent shares in this company which exists only on letter pads. From this point the minority shareholder started questioning, sending a series of complaints to SEBI, Income Tax, CBI, ED and Delhi Police Economic Offices Wing (EOW).

The minority shareholder unearthed the following deliberate violations in public limited company NDTV by the major promoter Prannoy Roy:

1. Covert acquisition by Promoters, Prannoy Roy and Radhika Roy of 8% equity from General Atlantic Partners in Dec 2007 and thereafter sale of over 15% equity to benami holders through a foreign fund – Goldman Sachs in Mauritius. This covert deal was a blatant violation of Stock Exchange rules and the two foreign investors were acting as partners in illegal trades and actions of Promoters. Finance Ministry under

P Chidambaram kept silent on this covert deal, as did SEBI, which is supposed to protect the interests of other shareholders.

2. Conspired with ICICI Bank and received funding of over ₹375 crores ($76 million) to husband and wife's private company RRPR Holdings Private Limited in the name of the public company NDTV. How ICICI Bank then under K V Kamath gave such a huge loan to shell company which is having no business, cash flows or assets is a million dollar question. The loan given by the bank was for consideration other than normal commercial basis and completely in violation of RBI Regulations. Thus ICICI Bank facilitated Mr. & Mrs. Roy and helped them retain control in NDTV, the public company in clear violation of RBI norms. This happened in October 2008 and the RBI buried this gross violation quietly. Not only was there a violation of RBI Regulations, but further a contravention of Banking Regulation Act and Prannoy Roy along with Radhika Roy, caused a loss of close to ₹50 crores to ICICI Bank when they forced the bank to settle the loan in August 2009. It is very strange as to why this has not been investigated by RBI and CBI as now private banks are also covered under the Prevention of Corruption Act.

Thereafter, in July 2009, ICICI Bank acted in concert/ facilitated Mukesh Ambani's Reliance Group and executed a clandestine agreement to take control of the news media company from Prannoy Roy and Radhika Roy. This was in complete violation of Ministry of Information and Broadcasting (MIB) norms, SEBI norms, Companies Act etc. and of course resulted in tax evasion to the tune of ₹300 crores ($61 million)[12]. However, what is a matter of intrigue and concern is the fact that even today it is not known who controls this news television network. Post Dec 2012, the ownership got transferred in a convoluted manner to a web of shell companies controlled by a Delhi based industrialist Mahendra Nahata, who was known as Ambani's man in Delhi.

Nahata is seen everywhere in most operations of Mukesh Ambani. Mahendra Nahata's telecom companies were always caught in scams from Sukh Ram scandals, 2G Scam and even Reliance Jio started business by a controversial move by acquiring a Nahata floated, little known company. It is quite possible that in 2012 the ownership (Nahata being a front) actually shifted from the elder Ambani brother to the younger – Anil Ambani as Mukesh by then had formalized and thereafter transferred ownership of another news network – TV18 group from Raghav Bahl. Some believe and it is rumored, that the two brothers agreed that one of the groups (NDTV) should change hands and thus the ownership was parked via a Special Purpose Vehicle - SPV (RRPR Holding P Ltd) with Mahendra Nahata.

During the period, June 2006 – October 2008 the media company floated many shell companies across global jurisdictions such as Sweden, Netherlands, UK, Mauritius and Dubai (over 30) etc. to bring into India via illegal hawala route a sum of over USD 150 million dollars. This is a clear case of violation of Income Tax Dept and ED provisions. After the execution of sham transactions many of these companies were closed. In some foreign companies, NDTV's prominent faces Barkha Dutt, Vikram Chandra and Suparna Singh were also shareholders or directors. All these companies were just paper companies at some hotel address or some attorney addresses. For more, see Figure 2 below:

Figure 2. Trail of NDTV Shell companies (Graphic: PGurus.com)

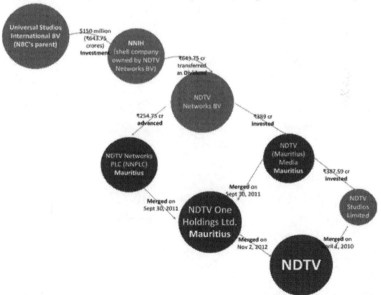

NDTV evaded over ₹500 crores of income tax and

laundered money through tax havens by floating many shell companies across the world[13]. SEBI shut their eyes on NDTV's money laundering and siphoning by promoters Prannoy Roy and wife Radhika Roy. MIB also kept silent when the shareholding pattern of the company was frequently changed.

When Sanjay Dutt and Jain came to know of the misdeeds, illegal acts and alleged frauds committed by the two promoters Radhika and Prannoy Roy, they decided to file a complaint with the Additional Commissioner of Police, Economic Offenses Wing, New Delhi. This was based on the findings of the Income Tax Dispute Resolution Panel (DRP), which in December 2013 had determined that NDTV, through its shell subsidiary companies colluded with National Broadcasting Corporation-Universal (NBCU), which was a subsidiary of the American giant General Electric (GE). What was striking about this investment was that NBCU transferred ₹584.46 crores to NDTV between 2008 and 2009 by purchasing shares in NNIH (an NDTV Shell company) Netherlands. But in the **next financial year**, the same shares were sold back to NDTV Networks BV, another NDTV shell company for a paltry sum of ₹58 crores, a loss of 90%! Why would a world reputed Multinational (MNC) company do this?

DRP saw through the ruse and arrived at the following conclusion: *"The only purpose apparent from the transaction is to create a loss of ₹584.46 crores for NBCU and to bring the taxable income of the assessee (NDTV) amounting to ₹642.54 crores, earned from undisclosed sources, into the books of accounts of the assessee through its subsidiaries."* Was this a creative way to bring its own (or benami for someone else) money back into India, with NBCU's help? That is what DRP concluded, which casts a harsh light on NBCU and its parent company GE for being a party in this sham transaction. Why would a reputed MNC invest $150 million in a shell company with **zero** employees and **zero** revenue?

It is pertinent to note that, in July 2009 while executing the illegal and clandestine change of control agreement to transfer ownership of the Media Company via sale of the holding (Khoka) company, the two promoters committed a breach of SEBI Regulations, Foreign Exchange Maintenance Act (FEMA) and Income Tax Act. In fact, the agreement shows that they knew they were committing PMLA violations and other SEBI Takeover code regulations. Most importantly, this has major security implications as MIB was neither informed nor permission taken to transfer control of a nationally sensitive news media company.

Round tripping of high value assets (Intellectual Property Rights (IPRs), Brand, inventories and media libraries) and also revenue streams of NDTV Ltd by the promoters of the Company to make an illegal gain of approximately ₹1200 crores ($243 million). This gain is distributed amongst the key Directors, Employees and others (Law Firms, CAs etc.) who facilitated/ validated these transactions. The money has been routed back into India through the Mauritius route of merger with an Indian entity without paying any short term or long term capital gains tax. Major NDTV promoter Prannoy Roy was ditching his 45,000 minor shareholders and siphoning and laundering the money into his private shell companies.

During the financial year FY 2008-2009, Prannoy Roy and Radhika Roy along with RRPR Holding Private Limited (RRPR) as Person Acting in Concert ("PAC"), in terms of Regulation 11(1) of the SEBI (Substantial Acquisition of Shares and Takeovers) Regulations, 1997 and subsequent amendments thereto ("SEBI (SAST) Regulations"), made a cash offer of Rs 438.98 per share of ₹4 each (the "Offer Price"), to acquire up to 1,26,90,257 fully paid Shares representing 20% of the Resulting Voting Share Capital ("Offer") of New Delhi Television Limited. It is important to note that RRPR did not own a single NDTV share before July 2008.

After July 2008, but in FY 2008-2009, the promoters increased their stake in NDTV and thereafter on August 5, 2009 partly divested their shareholding so as to enable RRPRHL to hold 26% in NDTV Ltd. The relevance of 26% is well known and established as a key control threshold level by various statutes.

The promoters, to meet the financing requirements for the said acquisition of shares of NDTV, took a loan of ₹500 plus crores from India Bulls Financial Services. Thereafter, during FY 2009-2010, ICICI Bank granted a loan of ₹375 crores in FY 2008 – 2009 and the loan of 'India Bulls Financial Services' was paid off by the promoters of NDTV Ltd. It is important to note that ICICI Bank loan was illegal and totally against the provision of Banking Regulations Act and Master Circular of RBI on Loans and Advance against shares to promoters of listed Companies. For this loan, the Promoters pledged, collateralized and created a non-disposal undertaking in favor of ICICI Bank for the entire 61% holding i. e. over 3.6 crores (36 million) shares in NDTV. Not only did they create a non-disposal undertaking, the Lawyers of the Promoters under their instructions have made a filing under affidavit (in the Delhi High Court) that all shares of the three Promoters were pledged/ collateralized in favor of ICICI Bank to secure the ₹375 crores loan. This act is not only illegal as per SEBI and RBI provisions, it also violates the basic licensing condition (as a broadcaster) as stipulated by Ministry of Information and Broadcasting. Those days UPA's MIBs Ambika Soni and Manish Tewari were frequenters to NDTV Studios. They could only watch when NDTV, blessed by Sonia Gandhi was creating all kinds of narratives as to why Rahul Gandhi should be the next Prime Minister of India.

During the same financial year FY 2009-2010, promoters paid back a substantial amount of ₹350 out of ₹375 crores through unsecured and interest free loan of ₹403.85 crores from a shell company linked to Reliance Industries Limited. The shell company's name is Vishwapradhan Commercial Private Ltd. (VCPL) and most of its Directors were staffers in Reliance Group.

After four years of a series of complaints to various agencies, in mid-2014, the minority shareholders knocked on the doors of judiciary[14]. Now Delhi High Court has ordered SEBI, ED, and IT to file responses on the complaints. The long arm of law has started catching up with NDTV and its promoters. Figure 3 shows all the filings QSL had to do to be heard by the various government agencies and courts:

Figure 3. Timeline of filings by Quantum Services Limited

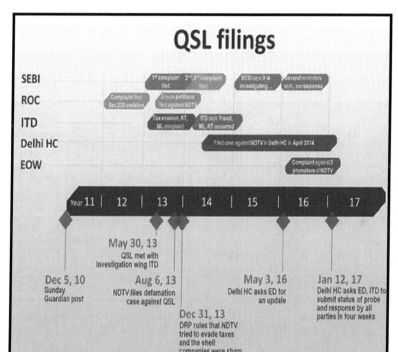

Table 3. Abbreviations explained

SEBI	Securities and Exchange Board of India
ROC	Registrar of Companies
ITD	Income Tax Department
RT	Round tripping
ML	Money Laundering
EOW	Economic Offences Wing
DRP	Dispute Resolution Panel of Income Tax Department

Some observations about the timeline graphic above:

1. QSL approached the Supreme Court on NDTV's defamation case and argued that the jurisdiction of Bombay High Court was because NDTV chose Mumbai with the sole intention of harassing them. The case is pending disposal and is currently frozen.

2. SEBI, since 2012-2013, has got several complaints relating to insider trading of the promoters, disclosure violations, fraudulent trades and take-over code violations from QSL but never bothered to even acknowledge them - forget taking action even after presentation of cogent evidence. Is it not the role of SEBI to ensure that the market is fair and gives equal opportunity for everyone to trade? How many times has SEBI punished the promoter of a publicly traded company? By law of averages, there will be crooks and SEBI's role is to catch them and punish them. It is easy to say that India has a vibrant stock market but if the watchdog organization does not act swiftly, it would turn investors away.

3. NDTV has about 45,000 small investors who perhaps, looking at the glitzy, honest sounding stars invested their hard-earned money into its shares and now are looking at utter ruin. Even if

NDTV is brought to book and an outside entity is appointed to auction off its assets, will the common man get his money back? Not only that, now that it has so many statutory liabilities from Income Tax and ED fines etc. piling up, what happens to the banks that may have given loans?

Did things improve after a change in government in May 2014? QSL wrote to the new Finance and Corporate Affairs Minister Arun Jaitley listing the frauds committed by the Promoters Radhika and Prannoy Roy. In a 15- page detailed letter dated Jun 6th, 2014 (copy also filed with the High Court), Sanjay Dutt, Director QSL explained with detail how his repeated queries to Promoters and inquires to Ministry of Corporate Affairs (MCA) and SEBI were ignored. After getting no response from the FM, Dutt again wrote to the Finance and Corporate Affairs Minister on October 20th, 2014, citing additional evidence found by two departments Enforcement Directorate and Income Tax (both of which come under Jaitley) and urged the Minister to act. However, as expected, no response from him on either of these letters or directions to his Departments to act.

Once QSL filed a writ petition in the Delhi High Court against NDTV in April 2014, agencies such as the ED and Income Tax began responding to specific queries. The reply by a Senior officer in the Office of Director General (DG) Investigation Income Tax dated Sept 11, 2015 confirmed that the Investigation Wing had investigated NDTV and its Promoters way back in 2011 with Netherlands and Cayman Islands into the tax affairs of NDTV group. In fact, in a document filed in the Delhi HC in September 2015 by DG Investigation (Income Tax), it is categorically stated that substantial tax was evaded by Prannoy Roy and Radhika Roy. Further, the affidavit also states that they received over ₹400 crores from a "bogus/khoka" company called Vishwapradhan Commercial Pvt. Ltd. However, what is intriguing is why has the department sat on this information for 5 years? It has not acted and neither has it shared this information relating to money laundering and unknown source of funds in a licensed news broadcaster with CBI for an investigation.

So all the information that was required to proceed against NDTV by CBI, ED and SEBI etc. was always with the government. Then why did UPA-2 do nothing? Further, why did the NDA-2 do nothing about it? It wasn't as if it was not reminded (it was, twice, in June and Oct 2014 i.e. letters to the FM). Until QSL filed a writ petition in Delhi High Court in 2014 and followed up every complaint diligently, the

Government chose to sit on its rather wide rear side and indulged in masterly inactivity. Pulling teeth might have been less painful for QSL as it did all the leg work that was the government's job. All this begs the question: Was the Lutyens cabal at work, trying to save one of their own? Remember who were employed at NDTV! Its not just political bosses with quid pro quo but also bureaucrats at SEBI and ED.

Chapter 6

Enforcement Directorate Catches NDTV

After Congress led UPA's exit, agencies started acting on a series of complaints filed against NDTV in several quarters, though Finance Minister Arun Jaitley did his best to stall. The first action came from Enforcement Directorate in early 2015. The ED officers found that NDTV had committed ₹2030 crores foreign exchange violations. But the attempts to send notice to NDTV under FEMA were blocked by many corrupt politicians and bureaucrats. Those days Rajan Katoch was the ED Chief and he was a UPA regime appointee and continuing in the organization getting one extension after another. Moreover this pliable officer was a cousin of the Congress leader Digvijaya Singh. Why BJP government gave him an extension is another question. Certain questions can't get simple answers in corrupt Lutyens Delhi which has opaque walls of mystery that some can walk through and others get their nose bloodied. That this cabal continues to cast a larger-than-life shadow on the Modi government shows the kind of power they wield among the *babulog*.

Social Media was abuzz with blockage of actions of ED by Finance Ministry top officials like the Revenue Secretary Shaktikanta Das, an acolyte of P Chidambaram. At last, after much nudging, the Prime Minister's office gave stern directions and Hasmukh Adhia became new Revenue Secretary and Karnal Singh became ED Chief. Subramanian Swamy and Gurumurthy were using their might for breaking the hidden designs of the Delhi's corrupt gang. Within weeks, in November 2015 the Enforcement Directorate under Karnal Singh slapped a notice on NDTV for laundering of ₹2030 crores.

The ED Investigation under FEMA has revealed that the financial transactions by NDTV Ltd were in total violation of RBI norms. In those days the RBI Governor Raghuram Rajan was a frequenter to NDTV Studios for giving exclusive interviews to Barkha Dutt. Rajan also played a part in scuttling the ED's probe[15] as part of the money from the Aircel-Maxis deal was routed through NDTV. ED's queries to RBI were mostly delayed and investigators had to force the bankers.

Following were the main violations by NDTV unearthed by ED. These violations were specified in the notice served to NDTV.

1. NDTV Ltd. through its step down subsidiary in UK, NDTV Networks Plc. (NNPLC) was permitted

by FIPB to raise overseas funds through public offerings of equity shares and allowed listing at London Stock Exchange and remit those funds in its group companies. But NNPLC raised funds by way of overseas loans, bonds and optionally convertible preference shares. NDTV Ltd. has violated Regulation 5 (1) of FEM (Transfer or Issue of Security to Persons resident outside India) Regulations, 2000 issued under Section 6 (3) (b) of FEMA by not complying with the terms and conditions of FIPB approval.

2. NDTV Ltd. raised funds outside India to the tune of USD 170 Million through NNPLC and brought USD 163.78 Million (₹725.56 crores approximately) in its group companies in India during the period March, 2007 to October, 2010. RBI has pointed out that bringing funds in its group companies by NDTV Ltd. from NNPLC is not a genuine and bonafide business activity and is a contravention of Regulation 6 (2)(ii) of the FEM (Transfer or Issue of any Foreign Security) Regulations, 2004 issued under Section 6 (3) (a) of FEMA.

3. NDTV Ltd. and its group companies in India further received USD 83,909,977 and USD 21,972 from its overseas subsidiaries namely NDTV Mauritius Media and NDTV Worldwide

Mauritius Ltd. under the automatic route of RBI in the guise of Foreign Direct Investment (FDI). RBI has pointed out that bringing funds in its group companies by NDTV Ltd. from its overseas subsidiaries is not a genuine and bonafide business activity and is a contravention of Regulation 6 (2)(ii) of the FEM (Transfer or Issue of any Foreign Security) Regulations, 2004. Thus, NDTV Ltd. received an amount of ₹1113.31 crores approximately in total in contravention of FEMA provisions.

4. NDTV Ltd. has issued Corporate Guarantees (CG) in favor of NNPLC to the tune of USD 84 Million relating to the arrangement of funds of USD 170 Million and loans taken by NNPLC which were not reported to RBI. RBI has pointed out that not seeking RBI approval and not reporting to RBI to issue a Corporate Guarantee is a contravention of Regulation 6(2)(vi) and Regulation 6(4) of the FEM (Transfer or Issue of any Foreign Security) Regulations, 2004.

5. NDTV Studios Ltd. (another group company of NDTV Ltd.) has deposited a sum of ₹200 crores with Bank of Baroda, Corporate Financial Branch, and Parliament Street, New Delhi relating to USD 70 Million Loan by NNPLC. NDTV Studios Ltd.

has contravened the provisions of Section 3 (d) of FEMA.

6. NDTV Ltd. bought back the transferred shares of its group companies namely NDTV Labs Limited, NDTV Imagine Limited, NDTV Convergence Limited, NDTV Lifestyle Limited and NGEN Media Services Ltd. to the tune of ₹296.74 crores from NNPLC to its group companies namely NDTV Lifestyle Holdings Limited and NDTV Networks Limited. RBI has pointed out that such transactions are in contravention of Regulation 6(2) (ii) of the FEM (Transfer or Issue of any Foreign Security) Regulations, 2004. Thus NDTV Ltd. has contravened this Regulation read with Regulation 10B of the FEM (Transfer or Issue of Security by a Person Resident outside India) Regulations, 2000, for the amount of ₹296.74 crores.

The ED's Show Cause Notice issued said that NDTV Ltd. has contravened the provisions of the above said provisions of FEMA and Regulations issued there under, in which the amount involved is around ₹2030.05 crores.

In the initial days NDTV tried to bully the ED sleuths. Only some accountants were sent to ED to give evasive replies. Flabbergasted, the ED officers warned the NDTV staffers, that they would summon Prannoy Roy. Then NDTV sent its CEO K V L Narayan Rao. Rao was questioned extensively by the ED and the Income Tax Department and after which he admitted that the rationale for setting up multiple shell companies abroad was only to circumvent the restrictions imposed by Indian regulations.

While all these covert deals, tax evasion, cross border "laundering structures" of dummy companies were created and more importantly Roys carried out a covert change of control, Independent Directors (who owe a fiduciary responsibility) looked the other way. NDTV has had the best names in Indian business as independent directors - Mr. N R Narayana Murthy of Infosys (who resigned in 2010) and Mr. Bhaskar Menon (former Chairman of record company EMI) who also resigned in 2016. In addition the ones who have continued on the Board are individuals like - Mr. Amal Ganguli (former Chairman of Price Waterhouse Coopers (PWC) India and Board member of many other public companies including some Tata companies), Mr. Pramod Bhasin (a very illustrious and well known founder of Genpact and a GE associate), Mr. Kaushik Datta (very strange, till 2011 was the signing partner of NDTV accounts being a PWC staffer and the statutory auditor). All these individuals have a lot of answering to do to its shareholders, SEBI, ED and now of course CBI and EOW. Mr. Datta is a more interesting one of the whole lot; he was the signing partner of RRPR Holding and NDTV at the same time when the alleged illicit change of control and controversial ICICI Bank loan was disbursed. Why did all these eminent individuals look the other way? Wasn't remaining silent meaning abetting all these acts of the Company and its Promoters? Why hasn't SEBI or the stock exchanges asked any questions from them?"

Subramanian Swamy was looking for an appropriate time to strike. In August 2016, he wrote to the Prime Minister that CBI should also register a case of cheating and conspiracy. His masterstroke was the demand of conversion of FEMA case to violations of PMLA (Prevention of Money Laundering Act). In FEMA, there was only fine. But in PMLA, the case is registered against persons along with companies and envisages jail term of three years to seven years. During the FEMA probe, ED can convert the case to PMLA, however, ED requires registration of a predicated offence or commonly known as a "Schedule Offence". This registration can only be done under specified laws such as IPC, SEBI Act and many other such laws. Now, it is incumbent on EOW

(Delhi Police), CBI and SEBI to register offences under the Schedule and thereafter, PMLA will be invoked by ED.

Swamy's main contention was that the major money laundering happened through a London based shell company of NDTV. He produced the directorship and shareholding pattern of the London based company NDTV Networks Plc. In this company apart from Mr. and Mrs. Roy, NDTV's senior journalists Barkha Dutt, Vikram Chandra and Suparna Singh were either shareholders and/ or directors (Annex 2). Swamy in his letter to Prime Minister Narendra Modi and Directors of CBI and ED argued that the case should be registered under the main faces of NDTV under PMLA (Swamy's complaint Annex 3).

In addition to Swamy, the petition filed by QSL (minority shareholder) before the Delhi HC wherein the ED and DG (Investigation) Income Tax are parties, it is clearly spelt out that PMLA should be invoked against RRPR Holding P Ltd. also as it has committed various violations covered under IPC, SEBI Act and Money Laundering.

ED also unearthed that NDTV have a 50 million dollar money trail during the Aircel-Maxis scam. The Investigation team led by Rajeshwar Singh had found that in 2006, the accused Malaysian company

Maxis had a money trail with NDTV, at the same period money from Maxis flown to Finance Minister P Chidambaram's son Karti's company Chess Management Private Limited.

After Swamy's case, many actors in the NDTV looting started changing their positions in the organization to save their skins. When the BJP government came to power, the first to change colors was Barkha Dutt who declared herself as a consulting staffer and started her own ventures. Vikram Chandra also changed his position from a managerial position. Is it like rats jumping first from the sinking ship? Prannoy Roy started staying mostly in his South African home. Is he going to be an absconder like fugitive Vijay Mallya and Lalit Modi? In fact, just a few weeks back, Barkha has completely washed her hands off NDTV and is not even associated with them as a consultant. One won't be surprised if Chandra does the same and many more high profile exits follow.

In the FEMA case, NDTV is expected to get a severe fine. But the nightmare for the NDTV leadership is when the ED decides to charge them under PMLA because in PMLA related cases, the minimum jail term is three years, ranging to a maximum of seven years, apart from the attachment of properties worth more than ₹2000 crores, leading to the shutting down of the corrupt empire built under the garb of journalism. In any case, it is time that the broadcasting license of NDTV be suspended (all channels taken off air) as SEBI has filed an affidavit in the Delhi HC in December 2016 clearly stating that as far back as August 2009, the Promoters (Radhika Roy and Prannoy Roy) in a clandestine arrangement took over ₹400 crores from VCPL and signed off control to the Reliance Group. This act itself is illegal as it is mandatory that no change of control of a media broadcaster can take place without MIB's specific permission.

Chapter 7

Income Tax Slaps ₹525 Crore On NDTV Frauds

After the eight years of tax fraud, NDTV was finally caught by the Income Tax Department in June 2016, after strict instructions from Prime Minister Narendra Modi's Office, removing the hurdles created by the Finance Minister Arun Jaitley. Income Tax sleuths slapped ₹525 crores fine on NDTV for illegally routing money through Bermuda and other tax havens in 2008. In fact, in addition to this the Department put together evidence along with a witness confirming that NDTV Promoters and key management along with advisors from PriceWaterhouse entered into "pre-meditated" tax fraud. It is after this that K.V.L. Narayan Rao (in September 2015) and now in February 2016, Vikram Chandra have been summoned and examined by the Tax Department.

ITD found that NDTV received unexplained money of ₹642,54,200 ($150 million)[13] from NBC Universal Inc and Universal Studios International BV in USA[13]. This money was routed through a shell company in Netherlands named NDTV Networks International Holdings BV to avoid paying income tax. Income

Tax sensed a fraud in 2010 when this transaction was suppressed in the statements submitted to it. That Assessment Year 2009-10 claimed ₹64 crores as loss! At that time the UPA-2 was in power and in strict adherence to coalition dharma, the Income Tax officers who questioned the covert money routing were silenced.

When Income Tax asked NDTV to explain how this ₹642 crores originated from America to Bermuda to Netherlands to India, NDTV gave curious and funny explanations that they were selling a "dream" and that the project would not succeed later.

The Income Tax officials noted in file that *"Assessee's (NDTV) theory of having sold a "Dream" to the investor has not been substantiated by any credible evidence as no details have been filed whatsoever for the so-called business projections and the basis of compulsion of the sale price of the share at the astronomical price of ₹7015 which is 159 times of its face value of ₹45. Needless to mention that the subject company whose shares were sold was incurring huge losses and there was hardly any worthy business to justify the above sale price."*

This illegal money routing happened in the second half of May 2008 during the UPA-1 tenure when Chidambaram was the Finance Minister. The 150 million dollars came from the US giant General Electrics' (GE) subsidiary NBC Universal Inc and Universal Studios International BV[13]. If it was a legitimate deal, the US Company would have to invest directly to NDTV's India office. But the GE's subsidiary invested money through its tax haven unit in Bermuda and NDTV received through its shell company in Netherlands to fool the Income Tax and other Indian agencies. The interesting part is that the shell company in Netherlands - NDTV Networks International Holdings BV – had just one person on its payroll. This man is shown as the CEO, Clerk, Peon etc. The multifaceted person was NDTV's Managing Editor Vikram Chandra, resident of India. The address was just a paid attorney's address in NDTV to fool the ITD. While doing this blatant fraud, NDTV continued to spout ethics and morality day after day! With slick English speaking anchors, the truth was buried and facts were twisted. Every officer who questioned the deal was mercilessly shot down by the system controlled by corrupt politicians and top officials from 2008 to 2015.

The company which received ₹640 crores unexplained money had the audacity to show ₹64 crores loss to Income Tax! There appears to be a hidden story behind this deal. Those days in 2006 to 2008, the US giant GE was trying to bag ₹16,000 crores ($3.74 billion) sweet deal from Indian Railways for creation of an Electrical Locomotive factory in the then Railway Minister Lalu Prasad Yadav's constituency in Madhepura. Though the word "electric" is in GE's name, GE was not an Electric Locomotive manufacturer. GE has only a Diesel Locomotive factory and they lost the tender in Railways for the Diesel Locomotive factory announced by Lalu at Marhowra in Bihar.

After losing the tender for Marhowra Diesel Locomotive factory implementation bid, GE tried every trick in the book to get the Madhepura Electrical Locomotive factory implementation bid. But there was a problem for GE as it was not an Electric Locomotive Engine manufacturer. The creative minions in GE produced false certificates to Indian Railways claiming that they are producing Locomotive Engines for Kyrgyzstan Railways, which was later caught red-handed in 2010 by Indian Railway officials. Was GE confused between Kyrgyzstan and Kazakhstan?[17] GE's legal team member Seema Sapra became a whistle-blower in this scam and was hounded and hunted.

A perusal of NDTV's annual reports from Fiscal Year 2008-2013 can be summarized using the following graphic:

Figure 4. Consolidated Financials of NDTV FY 2008-13

It can be easily seen that NDTV did not much care about their 45,000 shareholders. Every decision was directed at minimizing the tax footprint and enriching the pockets of a few individuals.

The timing of GE's subsidiary routing of 150 million dollar money to NDTV really needs investigation along with blatant frauds including alleged perjury committed by GE in trying to bag the ₹16,000 crores worth contract from Indian Railways. Are these two linked in some sort of a quid-pro-quo arrangement?

So how did GE end up investing in NDTV? Thereby appears to be another tale here. Planning Commission Member Montek Singh Ahluwalia was pushing for GE's ₹16,000 crores contract in Indian Railways and as usual many Cabinet Ministers were also supporting this deal. Needless to say that GE's proposals had the blessings of the then Finance Minister P Chidambaram. Without Finance Minister's support huge contracts worth more than ₹16,000 crore would not have seen the light of the day.

In reality, GE was trying to start its Locomotive Engine production facility using India's tax money without any expertise in the field. There was a huge quarrel among Planning Commission members on Montek Singh's move to push the deal towards GE. Some officers of Planning Commission found that though the deal was stated as Rs.16,000 crores, by the time it completes, the Indian Railways would have to shell more than ₹30,000 crores to the US giant GE. The deal fell through despite UPA-2 head Sonia Gandhi's blessings as from 2010 onwards, the country started witnessing a huge wave of anti-corruption movements after the exposure of 2G Scam. On November 9th, 2015, GE and Alstom signed a deal worth ₹40,000 crores for setting up Diesel and Electric Locomotive factories[18].

The Income Tax slapping of ₹525 crores for receiving money from GE's subsidiaries through a circuitous route has really affected NDTV. They never thought their eight year old crime would be caught. NDTV used its might to scuttle the Income Tax's action but failed due to the efforts of some honest officers. The case is now at the appeal stage at Income Tax Appellate Tribunal (ITAT) and the maximum NDTV can buy is time or perhaps a small reduction in fine. Paying this huge fine would certainly sound the death knell for the TV channel.

The detailed 14 page Income Tax notice slapping ₹525 crores fine is published. See Annex 4.

The Confession:

NDTV's CEO K V L Narayan Rao admitted to the fraud of floating a shell company in Netherlands to receive 150 million dollars in June 2016, after he was exhaustively questioned by the officers. Rao's confession is adequate grounds for Enforcement Directorate to register case for money laundering under PMLA, which envisages jail terms for the major players of NDTV frauds.

"In this regard, it is pertinent to mention that the statement of Mr. K V L Narayan Rao, Director of the assessee company (NDTV) and the then Group CEO, was recorded under on oath under section 131 of the Act on July 23, 2015, copy of which is enclosed. In this statement, in response to question No. 3, when asked about the rationale of incorporation of plethora of foreign subsidiaries, he admitted that "the foreign subsidiaries were incorporated to circumvent the restriction imposed by Indian regulations, which confined the foreign direct investment in news channel companies to a maximum of 26 percent," said an Income Tax Officer, on how 150 million dollar from US based GE Group company was flown illegally to NDTV through Netherlands. The 54 page document on this regard which includes the 33 page handwritten confession by Narayan Rao is available here[19].

The confession also exposes the shell companies floated by Prannoy Roy, wife Radhika Roy, Barkha Dutt, and Vikram Chandra abroad. These companies were just addresses of paid attorneys of those countries. Most of these paper companies were closed down by NDTV after various complaints were filed in 2010 onwards by several persons.

Chapter 8

Prannoy Roy And Wife Siphoned ₹146 Crores To Personal Accounts

There is a Chinese proverb: Never judge a person until the coffin is nailed. This suits Prannoy Roy, who became an icon due to the largesse of the public broadcaster Doordarshan. In 1998 he was caught by the CBI for cheating Doordarshan of around ₹5 crores. But all his contacts in Delhi saved him. But then he started looting his own baby NDTV.

He formed a shell company in his and wife's name – RRPR Holdings Private Limited somewhere in 2008. RRPR expands to Radhika Roy Prannoy Roy. This shell company was floated to loot the money he got in the name of NDTV, which is a public limited company listed on the Stock Exchange with more than 40,000 shareholders.

The ITD in December 2015 found that in October 2008 Prannoy Roy and wife siphoned ₹92 crores into their personal accounts. Soon Income Tax also found that in March 2010, Prannoy Roy siphoned another sum of around ₹54 crores to his personal account for a total of ₹146 crores.

First siphoning of ₹92 crores:

The Income Tax Department in December 2015 found that in October 2008, within two days of receiving ₹375 crores loan from ICICI Bank, Prannoy Roy diverted ₹21 crores to himself and ₹71 crores to wife Radhika Roy as interest free loans[20]. The role of ICICI Bank was also under controversy in this murky deal because the loan was allotted to the shell company RRPR Holdings Private Limited, which controls NDTV. There is little doubt that this dubious loan allotment to RRPR was given with the blessings of top ICICI Bank officials including its then head K V Kamath.

It is a matter of complete disbelief and points towards corruption (quid pro quo) or some other behind the scenes "sweet deal"... How is it possible for a Bank regulated by RBI to give a loan of ₹375 crores to a company that has a negative net worth, no earnings or cash flows and to top it all inadequate collateral? Shouldn't CBI be investigating this act of ICICI Bank along with the beneficiaries (Roys)?

RRPR is a shell company with no income having 50 percent shares each by husband and wife. Based on what collateral did ICICI Bank give the loan to a shell company? The loan with 19 percent interest was received on October 14, 2008, when NDTV's friend P

Chidambaram was the Finance Minister. On October 16, the RRPL grants interest free loan to its own Directors! This is nothing but fraud. It is sure that this was done with the blessings of ICICI Bank, which gave such a huge loan to a non-income showing shell company.

As per the Income Tax Report dated December 29, 2015, Prannoy Roy was granted interest free loan of ₹20,92,00,009 ($3.11 million)[21] by RRPL on October 16, 2008, just 48 hours after RRPL got ₹375 crores from ICICI Bank with 19 percent interest. The same day RRPL also gave interest free loan of ₹71,00,00,107 ($10.5 million) to wife Radhika Roy too. This implies that out of the ₹375 crores ($56 million) loan, ₹92 crores ($13.6 million) went to the Roy household! Prannoy Roy has been preaching integrity in public life for the longest time, as if he was always taking the high road. Irony died a thousand deaths[20]!

Another Income Tax Report of January 29, 2016 also details the complete fraudulent operations of Prannoy Roy through the shell company RRPL in controlling and bagging money in the name of Stock Exchange Listed Company NDTV.

Where was RBI those days on this dubious loan to a paper company? Well, P Chidambaram was the Finance Minister. That should explain how ICICI Bank gave such a loan and it was a fact that this news was published in M J Akbar owned Sunday Guardian[22], when Chidambaram was out of the Finance Ministry in December 2010. Those days there was a running feud going on between then Finance Minister Pranab Mukherjee and Home Minister P Chidambaram.

Delhi's people-in-the-know say that the dirty tricks department of an Industrial House leaked the ICICI Bank's dubious loan details to Akbar. The Industrial House owner was angry with his then quarreling brother for some hidden money funding in NDTV. The Industrial House owner had a feeling that certain news that appeared against him in NDTV was planted by his brother. Anyway many in Delhi had seen Akbar with the dirty tricks department head of the Industrial House owner many times during those days in late 2010. News always leaks in such a way that we don't need to go into how it is leaked and just focus on the message. To paraphrase P G Wodehouse, *one doesn't go about leaking one's secrets about one to one, does one?!* In fact, it is known in the Lutyens cabal that it was Pranab Mukherjee who brokered peace between Prannoy Roy and M J Akbar and along with this, a certain industrialist who was on the verge of being brought to book by CBI in the 2G scam also "cut a deal".

Income Tax report also exposes how Prannoy Roy's shell company told blatant lies to the Tax department. To the ITD they stated that they had attached bank transaction details and Certificates of Deposit (CD)s. But the ITD says that it was a total lie and they never attached any such documents. The detailed Income Tax reports are available at Annex 5.

Second siphoning of around ₹54 crores:

After stealing ₹92 crores from NDTV in October 2008, the next looting done by Prannoy Roy was on March 8, 2010. The Income Tax Department's sensitive report to Enforcement Directorate and Delhi Police Economic Offence Wing shows that around ₹54 crores was siphoned to the personal account of Prannoy Roy[23]. An exact amount of ₹53,84,60,960 was shifted from RRPR Holdings through a cheque number 84219 of Syndicate Bank (Hauz Khas Branch, Delhi) Account No: 10006971 to Prannoy Roy's account.

The money came to the shell company RRPR Holdings on March 8, 2010 from Mukesh Ambani's Reliance Group linked company VCPL for increasing the shareholding in NDTV from 26% to 29.19%.

IT also unearthed that on the same day in the Stock Exchange there were around ₹134 crores worth of transactions done at a price variation of 98%. The IT department found that these bogus gains were done to benefit the main promoters Mr. and Mrs. Roy and to enable RRPR Holding P Ltd to pay money out to the Roys that was in sync received from VCPL. The question that is on everyone's lips is when the Government is going to act against this instance of blatant Stock Exchange rigging.

In any other developed country if a major promoter siphons such a huge amount of money linked to a Stock Exchange listed company, he would have been in jail by now. But in India, the wheels of justice move slowly.

Chapter 9

Long Arm Of Law Catches Up With NDTV

At last the long arm of law has started catching up with NDTV. The wheels of justice started rolling when in November 28, 2016 the Delhi High Court ordered Stock Exchange Board of India (SEBI) to respond to a series of complaints filed by the minority shareholder Quantum Security Services Private Limited for the past four years. In a double whammy to NDTV, on January 12, 2017, Justice Sanjeev Sachdeva also ordered Enforcement Directorate and Income Tax Department to respond within four weeks about the complaints.

The Order passed on January 12 is a real nightmare to NDTV and its major players because, the High Court also ordered Enforcement Directorate and Income Tax Department to respond to other complaints filed by BJP leader Subramanian Swamy, journalist and financial analyst S Gurumurthy, former Chief Justice of India (CJI) R C Lahoti, former Finance Minister Yashwant Sinha, former top cop K P S Gill and whistle-blower Income Tax Commissioner S K Srivastava for the past few years.

This Order will force NDTV to face the CBI and Delhi

Police EOW probes as they are linked to the ongoing probes of Enforcement Directorate and Income Tax Department.

In addition to the January 12th order of the Delhi High Court, on January 17th, 2017, the Honorable Judge also ordered SEBI to file a reply as to why they have been refusing a hearing and submission of evidence in person by Quantum Securities P Ltd. This is the most bizarre situation - a **law enforcement agency is refusing** a deposition to an investor/ complaint who is privy to an act of crime and his statement and submissions would actually **assist the enforcement agency** to adjudicate the matter in a fair manner. One wonders as to why is SEBI avoiding this? Do they have instructions to **bury** these complaints and not let the complainant/ investor speak out the truth and depose under oath?

The confession of CEO K V L Narayan Rao (to the Income Tax Department) is going to affect NDTV badly. Rao's admission of guilt on illegally routing 150 million dollars in 2008 (at that time the value was ₹640 crores) through a Netherland based shell company is strong proof of money laundering and this would directly invite the slapping of charges under Prevention of Money Laundering Act (PMLA) which envisages jail term of three to seven years to the major players. Will Rao become an approver in Court to save his skin by sticking to the confession recorded before Income Tax officials? Only time will tell.

Who are the major players? Dr. Subramanian Swamy has already produced the London based shell company shareholding details involved in money laundering. Per the document (Annex 2), apart from Mr. and Mrs. Roy, senior journalists Barkha Dutt, Vikram Chandra and Suparna Singh are also shareholders or directors of the company during the scam period. Soon after money was laundered into India via the Mauritius routing, this paper company was closed. In fact, as per the annual report of NDTV, all these shareholders like Barkha and Vikram Chandra etc. received ex-gratia money from NDTV. Where does the minority shareholder or statutory dues such as income tax come in? Shouldn't they have received the legitimate taxes and dues before ex-gratia is distributed in a cash negative / loss making Company?

Now Barkha Dutt has jumped from the NDTV in second week of January 2017. There is a saying that rats will first jump from sinking ship. But in law, this jumping out is not an excuse or escape route. In criminal cases, those involved during the crime period have no excuse. She can save herself from criminal prosecution only by becoming an approver. Will she? Let us wait and watch.

Will Prannoy Roy and wife escape to their home in South Africa like the fugitives Vijay Mallya and Lalit Modi? For the past two years, many times Roy has flown to his South African home. This was the excuse given by his top officers to the Income Tax and Enforcement Directorate.

We must remember that NDTV in 2008 terminated around 500 staffers claiming a huge loss and blaming it on the Global Meltdown in USA. During this period they declared ₹64 crores to Income Tax and many persons faced salary cuts. But now facts prove that during the same period NDTV got 150 million dollars (worth ₹640 crores at that time) from GE's subsidiary company via Bermuda and Netherlands. Moreover on the same year Prannoy Roy and wife siphoned ₹92 crores to personal accounts. And this man preached ethics and morality!

NDTV from the very beginning was the product of an unholy nexus among journalists and politicians and with full encouragement of the latter; NDTV looted the resources of public broadcaster Doordarshan. From 2004, in many corruption cases, it can be seen that there is a money trail to NDTV. Be it Aircel-Maxis scam or GE's attempt to loot Indian Railways, somehow the key players in corruption either invested or routed money to NDTV's kitty. It is believed and known to many in the Lutyens circle that Prannoy Roy is a good friend of both T. Ananda Krishnan (of Astro Malaysia) and also of C. Sivasankaran. In fact, NDTV has done a few sweet deals with Astro and have received equity contribution from them. Were these part of a quid pro quo or are they genuine investment deals?

Niira Radia tapes expose how the controversial lobbyist helped pump money into NDTV. She was a key player in 2G Scam and the tapes exposed her role in hushing news of KG Basin looting. At the end we have seen all these players in the scam were investing or routing money in NDTV. Even one of the Coal Scam accused Naveen Jindal's father in law's company Oswal Group had invested in NDTV.

Forget the big scams, even in small incidents the NDTV management has taken their pound of flesh. In 2005-2006, there was a big strike in Honda plant in Haryana[24]. NDTV initially had hyped up the report as a big labour strike in Honda's car plant. But later it was seen that there was a heavy pumping of advertisements of Honda in NDTV and many senior staffers of NDTV were driving Honda Cars! How come all senior staffers were using the same car make? Staffers' excuse was that it was a part of a corporate arrangement through a soft loan provided by the company. Does this sound like a sweet quid pro quo between Honda and NDTV? These are all unethical activities in the garb of journalism. This kind of hit job or Supari journalism must cease for the benefit of the country and its democracy. Otherwise it would pollute the polity and society of the country. This must end.

There is a Latin saying frequently used in several judgments across the world – 'Fiat justitia ruat Caelum.' The meaning is - "Let justice be done though the heavens fall." This should happen. There is no point in shedding tears over the collapse of NDTV. The corrupt people headed by NDTV looted in the garb of the noble profession of journalism. And the corrupt must fall.

Once again let us repeat: 'Fiat justitia ruat Caelum.'

Footnotes

CHEATING FROM THE BEGINNING

1. The exchange rate in 1997 was on an average USD 1 = ₹35.75
2. The Tempest – How Radhika and Prannoy Roy undermined NDTV? Caravan Magazine December 1, 2015 issue
3. The 'Murdochization' of news? The case of Star TV in India by Daya Kishan Thussu

BEGINNING OF HIT JOBS AND UNETHICAL JOURNALISM

4. How Barkha Dutt helped the Terrorists – Excerpts from Gen. V P Malik's (Retd.) book Kargil – From Surprise to Victory
5. 2002Gujarat riots coverage by NDTV
6. NDTV Role in Adding Fuel to the Fire During 2002 Riots – Madhu Kishwar interviews Narendra Modi
7. Madhu Kishwar blasts Rajdeep Sardesai at Odisha Literary Festival
8. What is KG Basin Oil Scam?

MUZZLING THE WHISTLEBLOWER INCOME TAX OFFICER

9. CBI probes NDTV Tax assessment officers – PGurus website Aug 18, 2016
10. Average exchange rate was 1 USD = 43.40 rupees
11. The conversion rate used in this article is 1 USD = 66.89 Rupees

MINORITY SHAREHOLDER REVOLTS

12. The conversion rate used in this article is 1 USD = 49.33 Rupees
13. NDTV claimed they sold dreams. IT said: No. It is a sham transaction, slaps ₹525 cr fine – PGurus.com August 1, 2016

14. Writ Petition against SEBI on NDTV Documents filed in the High Court of Delhi by Quantum Securities

ENFORCEMENT DIRECTORATE CATCHES NDTV

15. Swamy seeks CBI-ED probe against NDTV and Prannoy Roy, Barkha Dutt, Vikram Chandra and Sonia Singh PGurus.com August 10, 2016

INCOME TAX SLAPS ₹525 CRORE ON NDTV FRAUDS

16. The conversion rate used is 1 USD = 42.80 Rupees
17. GE and Kazakhstan Temir Zholy (KTZ) Announce GE Evolution Series Passenger Locomotive to be Manufactured in Astana
18. GE, Alstom get contracts for Marhora, Madhepura loco projects Economic Times/ PTI Nov 9,2015
19. NDTV Director KVL Narayan Rao admits guilt of illegal money routing of $150M through Netherlands PGurus. com December 28, 2016

PRANNOY ROY AND WIFE SIPHONED ₹146 CRORES TO PERSONAL ACCOUNTS

20. Unending saga of NDTV frauds – Prannoy Roy & wife granted ₹92 crores interest free loan to themselves PGurus. com December 16, 2016
21. The conversion rate used in this article is 1 USD = 67.46 Rupees.
22. NDTV-ICICI loan chicanery saved Roys Sunday Guardian December 4, 2011
23. Prannoy Roy siphoned ₹53.84 crore to personal account from NDTV PGurus December 15, 2016

Index

Annexures

Annex 1: Income Tax findings against 2 IRS Officers

OFFICE OF SUPDT. OF POLICE
CENTRAL BUREAU OF INVESTIGATION
ANTI CORRUPTION UNIT - V
A - WING, 5-B, CGO COMPLEX,
NEW DELHI - 110003

No. 79·2 2172012A0002 CBI ACU(V)/New Delhi   Dated : -7 .08.2015

To,
The Principal Chief Commissioner of Income Tax (CCA)
3rd Floor, Central Revenue Building,
I.P.Estate,
New Delhi-110002.

Sub: Inquiry of Case PE 2172015A0002 CBI ACU(V)/New Delhi dated 10.06.2015 against
Mrs. Shumana Sen, the then ACIT, Range-13, New Delhi and others.

Sir,

This is in continuation of our earlier reference dated 16.06.2015 with regard to
registration of PE 2172015 A0005/CBI/ACU(V)/New Delhi against Mrs. Shumana Sen, the
then ACIT, Range-13, New Delhi and others.

2.   For the purpose of inquiry of the aforementioned case, the following additional
documents are urgently required:-

(i)   Certified copy of notice u/s 143(2) which was issued on 13.12.04 by Addl. CIT, R-13,
        Delhi and details of proceedings of first hearing reported to be commenced on
        21.12.04 before him in the matter of M/s NDTV Ltd. for the A.Y. 2004-05.

(ii)   Certified copy of all the files/recording on order sheets/assessment order about
        processing of return u/s 143(1), intimation issued and refund raised/issued for the
        A.Y. 2004-05 by the then DCIT, Circle-13(1), Delhi in the matter of M/s NDTV Ltd.

(iii)   Certified copy of letter No.842 dt. 28.03.05 from the O/o DCIT, Circle-13(1) seeking
        approval of the Addl. CIT, R-13 for issuance of refund on assessment record u/s
        143(1), alongwith recording to this effect on the order sheet, in the matter of M/s
        NDTV Ltd.   (The letter dt. 28.03.05 is part of the assessment records enclosed
        with the letter of the Addl. CIT, R-13, Delhi).

(iv)   Certified copies of jurisdiction of DCIT, Circle-13(1), Delhi to process the return u/s
        143(1), after case was taken up for scrutiny u/s 143(2) by the Addl. CIT, R-13, Delhi
        as per IT Act or other prevailing guidelines/orders in the matter of M/s NDTV Ltd.

(v)   Certified copies of guidelines/rules relating to Income Tax Act about the fact that
        whether more than one assessing officer can attend the same assessment
        proceedings for the same assessment year at the same time or simultaneously as
        in the case of M/s NDTV Ltd.

(vi)   Certified copy of intimation about employed status of spouse of Ms. Shumana Sen
        (the then DCIT, Circle-13, Delhi at the time of her joining in Govt. Service or

subsequent to her issuing processing order dt. 28.03.15 about refund of Rs. 1,46,82,836/- to M/s NDTV.

ii) The details of the declaration to the effect that Ms. Shumana Sen never had any official dealing with M/s NDTV Ltd. either at the time of obtaining permission for visiting U.K. in personal capacity on 12.04.05. or at the time of processing u/s 143(1) the case of M/s NDTV Ltd.

iii) Certified copy of notice u/s 148 dt. 28.3.12 and assessment order issued by AO for reassessment of income in respect of Ms. Shumana Sen and her husband Sh. Abhisar Sharma for different F.Y and A.Y., in the matter of her private visits abroad.

x) Certified copy of order dated 30.03.15 u/s 263 of IT Act issued by Principal Commissioner of IT in respect of Ms. Shumana Sen, order dated 30.03.15 u/s 263 of IT Act issued by Principal Commissioner of IT in respect of Sh. Abhisar Sharma, husband of Ms. Shumana Sen, assessment order u/s 143(3) and 147/148 for the A.Y 2007-2008 in respect of both Ms. Shumana Sen and her husband Sh. Abhisar Sharma and other orders with regard to escaped assessment of Income Tax by IT Deptt., alongwith supporting documents, submitted by her about her claims about her visit abroad filed before the departmental authorities.

x) Certified copy of letter dt. 17.10.11 wherein Ms. Shumana Sen had submitted before departmental authorities that the expenditure involved on her foreign travels was part of salary package of Sh. Abhisar Sbarma her husband from the employer of Sh. Ahishar Sharma i.e. M/s NDTV Ltd., alongwith all the case records/affidavits/judgements relating to Hon'ble High Court in CWP No. 4022/12 and other subsequent writ petitions filed by Ms. Shumana Sen against her reassessment.

xi) Certified copy of all the appraisal reports including wealth tax report prepared in respect of M/s NDTV Ltd. under Income Tax Act, 1961 alongwith all the files/recording on order sheets etc.

xii) Certified copy of judgement by the Hon'ble Supreme Court of India in the case of CIT Vs. Gujarat Electricity Board (2003) 260 ITR 84 wherein the Hon'ble Supreme Court has held that summary assessment u/s 143(1) cannot be resorted to after proceedings for regular assessment u/s 143(2) has commenced. The other guidelines/orders/Acts preventing passing the order u/s 143(1) after cases were taken up u/s/ 143(2) of IT Act.

5. It is, therefore, requested to kindly provide the aforesaid documents to Sh. Lalit Phular, Inspector, CBI, ACU-V, New Delhi(Mobile no. 9650094485) latest by 14.08.2015 positively who is the inquiry officer of this case.

This may kindly be treated as MOST URGENT.

Yours faithfully,

07.08.15

(Pradip Kumar)
Supdt. Of Police

OFFICE OF SUPDT. OF POLICE
CENTRAL BUREAU OF INVESTIGATION
ANTI CORRUPTION UNIT · V
A · WING, 5-B, CGO COMPLEX,
NEW DELHI · 110003

REMINDER

No· |||... /PE2172015A0002 CBI ACU(V)/New Delhi   Dated : ...03.2016

To,

The Principal Chief Commissioner of Income Tax (CCA)
3rd Floor, Central Revenue Building,
I.P.Estate,
New Delhi-110002.

Sub: Inquiry of Case PE 2172015A0002 CBI ACU(V)/New Delhi dated 10.06.2015 against Mrs. Shumana Sen, the then ACIT, Range-13, New Delhi and others.

Sir,

Please refer to this office letter No. 10026/PE2172015A0002/ CBI/ACU(V)/ND dated 27.10.2015 followed by reminder dated 22.01.16 on the aforementioned subject.

2. In this connection, the requisite information/documents with regard to granting permission for foreign visit to Ms. Shumana Sen, the then ACIT and other relevant documents as called for by this office may immediately be supplied to CBI for taking further action in the matter.

Yours faithfully,

(Ajay Kumar)
Supdt. Of Police
CBI/ACU-V/New Delhi

85

Annex 2: Directorship and shareholding pattern of
the London based company NDTV Networks Plc.

FILE COPY

CERTIFICATE OF INCORPORATION

OF A PUBLIC LIMITED COMPANY

Company No.   6015161

The Registrar of Companies for England and Wales hereby certifies that

NDTV NETWORKS PLC

is this day incorporated under the Companies Act 1985 as a public
company and that the company is limited.

Given at Companies House, London, the 30th November 2006

N060151617

THE OFFICIAL SEAL OF THE
REGISTRAR OF COMPANIES

Companies House

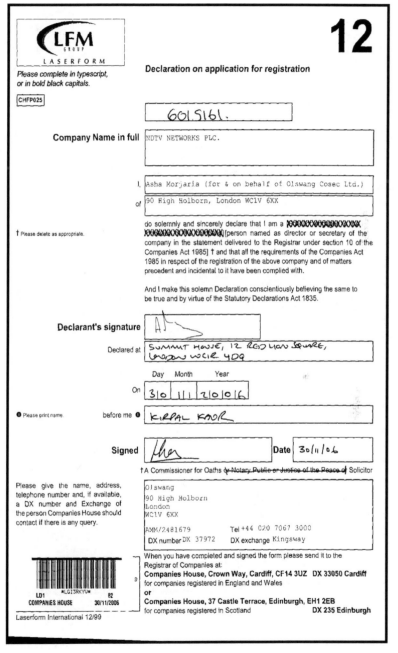

12

LFM
GROUP
LASERFORM

Please complete in typescript,
or in bold black capitals.

CHFP025

Declaration on application for registration

601 5161.

Company Name in full NDTV NETWORKS PLC.

I, Asha Morjaria (for & on behalf of Olswang Cosec Ltd.)

of 90 High Holborn, London WC1V 6XX

do solemnly and sincerely declare that I am a XXXXXXXXXXXXXXXXXXXXX
XXXXXXXXXXXXXXXXXXXXX [person named as director or secretary of the
company in the statement delivered to the Registrar under section 10 of the
Companies Act 1985] † and that all the requirements of the Companies Act
1985 in respect of the registration of the above company and of matters
precedent and incidental to it have been complied with.

† Please delete as appropriate.

And I make this solemn Declaration conscientiously believing the same to
be true and by virtue of the Statutory Declarations Act 1835.

Declarant's signature

Declared at SUMMIT HOUSE, 12 RED LION SQUARE,
LONDON WC1R 4DQ

Day Month Year

On 3 0 1 1 2 0 0 6

❶ Please print name.

before me ❶ KIRPAL KAUR

Signed Date 30/11/06

†A Commissioner for Oaths ~~or Notary Public or Justice of the Peace~~ of Solicitor

Please give the name, address,
telephone number and, if available,
a DX number and Exchange of
the person Companies House should
contact if there is any query.

Olswang
90 High Holborn
London
WC1V 6XX

AMM/2481679   Tel +44 020 7067 3000

DX number DX 37972   DX exchange Kingsway

When you have completed and signed the form please send it to the
Registrar of Companies at:
Companies House, Crown Way, Cardiff, CF14 3UZ DX 33050 Cardiff
for companies registered in England and Wales
or
Companies House, 37 Castle Terrace, Edinburgh, EH1 2EB
for companies registered in Scotland   **DX 235 Edinburgh**

LD1   82
COMPANIES HOUSE   30/11/2006

LGI3RKYU

Laserform International 12/99

87

NDTV FRAUDS

10

First directors and secretary and intended situation of registered office

6015161

Company Name in full

NDTV NETWORKS PLC.

Proposed Registered Office

(PO Box numbers only, are not acceptable)

SEVENTH FLOOR

90 HIGH HOLBORN

Post town | LONDON

County / Region | | Postcode | WC1V 6XX

If the memorandum is delivered by an agent for the subscriber(s) of the memorandum mark the box opposite and give the agent's name and address.

Agent's Name

Address

Post town

County / Region | | Postcode

Number of continuation sheets attached

You do not have to give any contact information in the box opposite but if you do, it will help Companies House to contact you if there is a query on the form. The contact information that you give will be visible to searchers of the public record.

Olswang
90 High Holborn
London
WC1V 6XX
AMM/2481338   Tel +44 020 7067 3000
DX number DX 37972   DX exchange Kingsway

When you have completed and signed the form please send it to the Registrar of Companies at:

Companies House, Crown Way, Cardiff, CF14 3UZ   DX 33050 Cardiff
or companies registered in England and Wales   or
Companies House, 37 Castle Terrace, Edinburgh, EH1 2EB
or companies registered in Scotland   DX 235 Edinburgh

88

Company Secretary (see notes 1-5)

Company name: NDTV NETWORKS PLC.

NAME   *Style / Title: *Honours etc

* Voluntary details

Forename(s): OLSWANG COSEC LIMITED

Surname:

Previous forename(s):

†† Tick this box if the address shown is a service address for the beneficiary of a Confidentiality Order granted under section 723B of the Companies Act 1985 otherwise, give your usual residential address. In the case of a corporation or Scottish firm, give the registered or principal office address.

Previous surname(s):

Address ††: SEVENTH FLOOR

90 HIGH HOLBORN

Post town: LONDON

County / Region: Postcode: WC1V 6XX

Country:

I consent to act as secretary of the company named on page 1

Consent signature   Date: 30|11|2006

FOR AND ON BEHALF OF OLSWANG COSEC LIMITED

Directors (see notes 1-5)

Please list directors in alphabetical order

NAME   *Style / Title: MRS   *Honours etc

Forename(s): RADHIKA

Surname: ROY

Previous forename(s):

†† Tick this box if the address shown is a service address for the beneficiary of a Confidentiality Order granted under section 723B of the Companies Act 1985 otherwise, give your usual residential address. In the case of a corporation or Scottish firm, give the registered or principal office address.

Previous surname(s):

Address ††: B-207, GREATER KAILASH-I

Post town: NEW DELHI

County / Region: Postcode: 110048

Country: INDIA

Day	Month	Year
0 9	0 7	1 9 4 9

Date of birth   Nationality: INDIAN

Business occupation: JOURNALIST

Other directorships: NONE

I consent to act as director of the company named on page 1

Consent signature   Date: 30|11|2006

89

Company Secretary (see notes 1-5)   Form 10 Continuation Sheet

| CHFP025 | | Company name | NDTV NETWORKS PLC. |

| | **NAME** | *Style / Title | | *Honours etc | |

* Voluntary details

| | Forename(s) | |

| | Surname | |

| | Previous forename(s) | |

| | Previous surname(s) | |

†† Tick this box if the address shown is a service address for the beneficiary of a Confidentiality Order granted under section 723B of the Companies Act 1985 otherwise, give your usual residential address. In the case of a corporation or Scottish firm, give the registered or principal office address

	Address ††	
	Post town	
	County / Region		Postcode	
	Country	

I consent to act as secretary of the company named on page 1

| | **Consent signature** | | Date | |

Directors (see notes 1-5)

Please list directors in alphabetical order

| | **NAME** | *Style / Title | MR | *Honours etc | |

| | Forename(s) | KOTIKALAPUDI VENKATA LAKSHMI NARAYAN |

| | Surname | RAO |

| | Previous forename(s) | |

| | Previous surname(s) | |

†† Tick this box if the address shown is a service address for the beneficiary of a Confidentiality Order granted under section 723B of the Companies Act 1985 otherwise, give your usual residential address. In the case of a corporation or Scottish firm, give the registered or principal office address

	Address ††	26, 2ND FLOOR, NRI COMPLEX,
		MANDAKINI
	Post town	NEW DELHI
	County / Region		Postcode	110019
	Country	INDIA

| | | Day | Month | Year | | |
| **Date of birth** | | 0 9 | 0 4 | 1 9 5 4 | **Nationality** | INDIAN |

| **Business occupation** | SERVICE |

| **Other directorships** | NONE |

I consent to act as director of the company named on page 1

| | **Consent signature** | [signature] | Date | 30|11|2006 |

Laserform International 6/02

AMM/2481362

248136

Company Secretary (see notes 1-5)

NAME *Style / Title [ ] *Honours etc [ ]

* Voluntary details

Forename(s) [ ]

Surname [ ]

Previous forename(s) [ ]

Previous surname(s) [ ]

†† Tick this box if the address shown is a service address for the beneficiary of a Confidentiality Order granted under section 723B of the Companies Act 1985 otherwise, give your usual residential address. In the case of a corporation or Scottish firm, give the registered or principal office address

Address †† [ ]

Post town [ ]

County / Region [ ] Postcode [ ]

Country [ ]

I consent to act as secretary of the company named on page 1

Consent signature [ ] Date [ ]

Directors (see notes 1-5)

Please list directors in alphabetical order

NAME *Style / Title MR *Honours etc [ ]

Forename(s) VIKRAMADITYA

Surname CHANDRA

Previous forename(s) [ ]

Previous surname(s) [ ]

Address †† C-4/2, I FLOOR

VISANT VIHAR

Post town NEW DELHI

County / Region [ ] Postcode [ ]

Country INDIA

Day Month Year

Date of birth 0 1 0 7 1 9 6 7 Nationality INDIAN

Business occupation JOURNALIST

Other directorships NIL

I consent to act as director of the company named on page 1

Consent signature [signature] Date 30|11|2006

24813

91

NDTV FRAUDS

Directors (see notes 1-5)
Please list directors in alphabetical order

| | NAME | *Style / Title | DR | | *Honours etc | |

* Voluntary details

Forename(s) | PRANNOY

Surname | ROY

Previous forename(s) |

Previous surname(s) |

†† Tick this box if the address shown is a service address for the beneficiary of a Confidentiality Order granted under section 723B of the Companies Act 1985 otherwise, give your usual residential address. In the case of a corporation or Scottish firm, give the registered or principal office address.

Address †† | B-207, GREATER KAILASH-I

Post town | NEW DELHI

County / Region | | Postcode | 110048

Country | INDIA

	Day	Month	Year		
Date of birth	1 5	1 0	1 9 4 9	Nationality	INDIAN

Business occupation | ECONOMIST

Other directorships | NONE

I consent to act as director of the company named on page 1

Consent signature | *[signature]* | Date | 30 11 2006

This section must be signed by

Either

an agent on behalf of all subscribers | Signed | *[signature]* | Date | 30 11 2006

Or the subscribers | Signed | *[signature]* | Date | 30 11 2006

(i.e those who signed as members on the memorandum of association). | Signed | | Date |

| Signed | | Date |

| Signed | | Date |

| Signed | | Date |

| Signed | | Date |

No.

6015161

3 0

£50 FEE PAID
COMPANIES
HOUSE

639333

THE COMPANIES ACT 1985 AND 1989

PUBLIC COMPANY LIMITED BY SHARES

MEMORANDUM OF ASSOCIATION

- of -

NDTV NETWORKS PLC.

1. The Company's name is NDTV Networks PLC.

2. The Company is to be a Public Company.

3. The Company's registered office is to be situated in England and Wales.

4. The Company's objects are:

4.1 to carry on business as a general commercial company; to carry on all or any of the businesses of general merchants and traders, manufacturers, assemblers, distributors, importers, exporters, merchants, factors, and shippers of, and wholesale and retail dealers in, goods, wares produce, products, commodities, fancy goods, handicrafts, and merchandise of every description, to act as agents for and to enter into agreements and arrangements of all kinds on behalf of such persons, firms or companies as may be thought expedient, and to negotiate, assign and mortgage or pledge for cash or otherwise, any such agreements and the payments due thereunder and any property the subject thereof, to carry on all or any of the businesses of mail order specialists, credit and discount traders, cash and carry traders, manufacturers' agents, commission and general agents, brokers, factors, warehousemen, and agents in respect of raw materials and manufactured goods of all kinds, and general railway, shipping and forwarding agents and transport contractors; to create, establish, build up, and maintain an organisation for the marketing, selling, retailing, servicing, advertisement, distribution or introduction of the products, merchandise, goods, wares, and commodities dealt in or services rendered by any person, firm or company, and to participate in, undertake, perform and carry out all kinds of commercial, trading and financial operations and all or any of the operations ordinarily performed by import, export and general merchants, factors, shippers, agents, traders, distributors, capitalists and financiers, either on the Company's own account or otherwise; and to open and establish shops, stalls, stores, markets and depots for the sale, collection and distribution of the goods dealt in by the Company;

2481401-1   1

4.2   to carry on any other trade or business whatsoever which, in the opinion of the board of directors of the Company, may be capable of being advantageously carried on by the Company in connection with or ancillary to any other business of the company, or may further any of the Company's objects;

4.3   to carry on the business of a holding company in all its branches and to co-ordinate the policy and administration of any subsidiary company of the Company or of any company of which the Company is a member or which is in any manner controlled by the Company;

4.4   to purchase, take on lease or in exchange, hire or otherwise acquire and hold any estate or interest in any lands, buildings, easements, rights, privileges, concessions, patents, patent rights, licences, secret processes, machinery, plant, stock-in-trade, and any real or personal property of any kind for such consideration and on such terms as may be considered expedient;

4.5   to erect, construct, lay down, enlarge, alter and maintain any roads, railways, tramways, sidings, bridges, reservoirs, shops, stores, factories, buildings, works, plant and machinery necessary or convenient for the Company's business, and to contribute to or subsidise the erection, construction and maintenance of any of the above;

4.6   to borrow or raise or secure the payment of money for the purpose of or in connection with the Company's business, and for the purposes of or in connection with the borrowings or raising of money by the Company to become a member of any building society;

4.7   to lend and advance money or give credit on any terms with or without security to any company or firm or person (including without limitation any holding company or subsidiary or fellow subsidiary of or any other company associated in any way with the Company), to enter into guarantees and contracts of indemnity and suretyships of all kinds, to receive money on deposit or loan upon any terms, and to secure or guarantee in any manner and upon any terms the payment of any sum of money or the performance of any obligation by any company or firm or person (including without limitation any holding company or subsidiary or fellow subsidiary or associated company);

4.8   to mortgage and charge the undertaking and all or any of the real and personal property and assets, present or future, and all or any of the uncalled capital for the time being of the company, and to issue at par or at a premium or discount, and for such consideration and with and subject to such rights, powers, privileges and conditions as may be thought fit, debentures or debenture stock, either permanent or redeemable or repayable, and collaterally or further to secure any securities of the Company by a trust deed or other assurance;

4.9   to issue and deposit any securities which the Company has power to issue by way of mortgage to secure any sum less than the nominal amount of such securities, and also by way of security for the performance of any contracts or obligations of the Company or of its customers or other persons or corporations having dealings with the Company, or in whose businesses or undertakings the Company is interested, whether directly or indirectly;

4.10 to receive money on deposit or loan upon such terms as the Company may approve, and to guarantee the obligations and contracts of any person or corporation;

4.11 to make advances to customers and others with or without security and upon such terms as the Company may approve, and generally to act as bankers for any person or corporation;

4.12 to grant pensions, allowances, gratuities and bonuses to officers, ex-officers, employees or ex-employees of the Company or its predecessors in business or the dependants or relations of such persons, to establish and maintain or concur in establishing and maintaining trusts, funds or schemes (whether contributory or non-contributory) with a view to providing pensions or other benefits for any such persons as aforesaid, their dependants or relations, and to support or subscribe to any charitable funds or institutions, the support of which may, in the opinion of the Directors, be calculated directly or indirectly to benefit the company or its employees, and to institute and maintain any club or other establishment or profit sharing scheme calculated to advance the interests of the Company or its officers or employees;

4.13 to draw, make, accept, endorse, negotiate, discount and execute promissory notes, bills of exchange and other negotiable instruments;

4.14 to invest and deal with the moneys of the Company not immediately required for the purposes of its business in or upon such investments or securities and in such manner as may from time to time be determined

4.15 to pay for any property or rights acquired by the Company, either in cash or fully or partly paid-up shares, with or without preferred or deferred or special rights or restrictions in respect of dividend, repayment of capital, voting or otherwise, or by any securities which the Company has power to issue, or partly in one mode and partly in another, and generally on such terms as the Company may determine;

4.16 to accept payment of any property or rights sold or otherwise disposed of or dealt with by the Company, either in cash, by instalments or otherwise, or in fully or partly paid-up shares of any company or corporation, with or without deferred or preferred or special rights or restrictions in respect of dividend, repayment of capital, voting or otherwise, or in debentures or mortgage debentures or debenture stock, mortgages or other securities of any company or corporation, or partly in one mode and partly in another, and generally on such terms as the Company may determine, and to hold, dispose of or otherwise deal with any shares, stock or securities so acquired;

4.17   to enter into any partnership or joint-purse arrangement or arrangement for sharing profits, union of interest or co-operation with any company, firm or person carrying on or proposing to carry on any business within the objects of this Company, and to acquire and hold, sell, deal with or dispose of shares, stock or securities of any such company, and to guarantee the contracts or liabilities of, or the payment of the dividends, interest or capital of any shares, stock or securities of and to subsidise or otherwise assist any such company;

4.18   to establish or promote or concur in establishing or promoting any other company whose objects shall include the acquisition and taking over of all or any of the assets and liabilities of the Company or the promotion of which shall be in any manner calculated to advance directly or indirectly the objects or interests of the Company, and to acquire and hold or dispose of shares, stock or securities of and guarantee the payment of the dividends, interest or capital of any shares, stock or securities issued by or any other obligations of any such company;

4.19   to purchase or otherwise acquire and undertake all or any part of the business, property, assets, liabilities and transactions of any person, firm or company carrying on any business which the Company is authorised to carry on;

4.20   to sell, improve, manage, develop, exchange, let on lease or otherwise, mortgage, charge, sell, turn to account, grant licences options, easements and other rights in or over, and in any other manner deal with or dispose of the undertaking and all or any of the property and assets for the time being of the Company for such consideration as the Company may think fit;

4.21   to amalgamate with any other company whose objects are to include objects similar to those of this Company, whether by sale or purchase (for fully or partly paid-up shares or otherwise) of the undertaking, subject to liabilities of this or any such other company as aforesaid, with or without winding up, or by sale or purchase (for fully or partly paid-up shares or otherwise) of all or a controlling interest in the shares or stock of this or any such other company as aforesaid, or in any other manner;

4.22   to distribute among the members in specie any property of the Company, or any proceeds of sale or disposal of any property of the Company, but so that no distribution amounting to a reduction of capital be made except with the sanction (if any) for the time being required by law;

4.23   to do all or any of the above things in any part of the world, and either as principal, agent, trustee, contractor or otherwise, and either alone or in conjunction with others, and either by or through agents, trustees, sub-contractors or otherwise;

4.24   to do all other things as are incidental or conducive to the attainment of the Company's objects or any of them.

2481401-1   4

None of the objects set out in any sub-clause of this clause shall be restrictively construed and the widest interpretation shall be given to each object. The word "company" in this clause, except where used in reference to the Company, shall be deemed to include any partnership, body corporate or unincorporated association whether domiciled in the United Kingdom or elsewhere. None of the objects shall, except where the context expressly requires, be in any way limited by or restricted by reference to or inference from any other object or objects set out in that sub-clause or by reference to or inference from the terms of any other sub-clause of this clause or by reference to or inference from the name of the Company.

5. The liability of the members is limited.

6. The share capital of the Company is £40,000,000 divided into 400,000,000 ordinary shares of £0.10p each.

NDTV FRAUDS

We, the subscriber to this Memorandum of Association, wish to be formed into a company pursuant to this Memorandum and we agree to take the number of shares shown opposite our name.

NAME AND ADDRESS OF SUBSCRIBER	Number of shares taken by each subscriber
New Delhi Television Ltd. W-17, Greater Kailash-I New Delhi 110048 Delhi India	One *(signature)* for and on behalf of New Delhi Television Ltd.
NDTV Investments Pvt. Ltd W-17, Greater Kailash-I New Delhi 110048 Delhi India	One *(signature)* for and on behalf of NDTV Investments Pvt. Ltd

Dated this 30 day of November 2006

Witness to the above signature: *(signature)*

Name: Sudhanshu Kumar Singh

Address: D-207, Okhla Industrial Estate, Phase-III, New Delhi-110020

Occupation: Service

2481401-1   6

No. 5114893

THE COMPANIES ACTS 1985 AND 1989

PUBLIC COMPANY LIMITED BY SHARES

ARTICLES OF ASSOCIATION

OF

NDTV NETWORKS PLC.

1.   INTERPRETATION

1.1   In these Articles the expression "Table A" means Table A in the Schedule to the Companies (Tables A to F) Regulations 1985 as amended by the Companies (Tables A to F) (Amendment) Regulations 1985.

1.2   Save as otherwise provided in these Articles, words and expressions which have particular meanings in Table A shall have the same respective meanings in these Articles.

1.3   Wherever in Table A or in these Articles any notice, resolution or other document is required to be signed by any person the reproduction of the signature of such person by means of telex print-out or facsimile copy shall be fully sufficient, provided that such notice, resolution or document shall within 14 days be confirmed to the recipient by writing signed in manuscript by such person.

1.4   In Table A and in these Articles, references to writing shall include any method of representing or reproducing words in a legible and non-transitory form.

1.5   References herein to Articles are to the numbered paragraphs of these Articles and to Regulations are to the regulations of Table A.

2.   ADOPTION OF TABLE A

2.1   The Company is a public company. The Regulations contained in Table A shall (except where they are excluded or modified by these Articles) apply to the Company and, together with these Articles, shall constitute the Articles of the Company.

2.2   Subject to Article 2.1, no regulations scheduled to any statute concerning companies shall apply to the Company.

3.   ALLOTMENT AND ISSUE OF SHARES

3.1   Subject to the Act and to any direction to the contrary which may be given by ordinary or other resolution of the Company, any unissued shares of the Company (whether forming part of the original or any increased capital) shall be at the disposal of the directors who may offer, allot

99

(with or without conferring a right of renunciation), grant options over or otherwise dispose of the same to such persons, at such times, and generally on such terms and conditions as they may determine.

3.2   Subject to the provisions of the Act, the directors are generally and unconditionally authorised for the purposes of section 80 of the Act to exercise any power of the Company to allot (as defined for the purposes of such section) all relevant securities (as defined for such purposes) of the Company subsisting at the date of incorporation at any time or times during the period of 5 years from such date.

3.3   At the expiry of such period of 5 years, the authority contained in Article 3.2 shall expire but such authority shall permit the directors to make any offer or agreement before the expiry of such authority which would or might require relevant securities to be allotted, or rights to subscribe for or to convert any security into shares to be granted, after the expiry of such authority.

3.4   Section 89(1) of the Act shall not apply to the allotment by the Company of equity securities pursuant to the general authority granted by Article 3.2.

4.   REDEEMABLE SHARES

Subject to the provisions of the Act, shares may be issued which are to be redeemed or are to be liable to be redeemed at the option of the Company or the member. Regulation 3 shall not apply.

5.   PURCHASE OF OWN SHARES

Subject to the provisions of the Act, the Company may enter into any contract for the purchase of all or any of its shares of any class (including any redeemable shares) and any contract under which it may, subject to any conditions, become entitled or obliged to purchase all or any such shares and may make payments in respect of the redemption or purchase of such shares otherwise than out of distributable profits or the proceeds of a fresh issue of shares. Every contract entered into pursuant to this Article shall be authorised by such resolution of the Company as may for the time being be required by law but subject thereto the directors shall have full power to determine or approve the terms of any such contract. Neither the Company nor the directors shall be required to select the shares in question rateably or in any other particular manner as between the holders of shares of the same class or as between them and the holders of shares of any other class or in accordance with the rights as to dividends or capital conferred by any class of shares. Subject to the provisions of the Act, the Company may agree to the variation of any contract entered into pursuant to this Article and to the release of any of its rights or obligations under any such contract. Notwithstanding anything to the contrary contained in the Articles, the rights attaching to any class of shares shall not be deemed to be varied by anything done by the Company pursuant to this Article. Regulation 35 of Table A shall not apply.

2

6. CALLS

The liability of any person in default in respect of a call shall be increased by the addition at the end of the first sentence of Regulation 18 of the words "and all expenses that may have been incurred by the Company by reason of such non-payment.".

7. TRANSFER OF SHARES

7.1 No share shall be transferred, assigned, charged or otherwise disposed of without the prior written consent of all the members. Regulation 24 shall not apply.

7.2 The directors shall, subject to its being properly stamped, forthwith register any transfer to which all the members for the time being of the Company shall have assented in writing and shall not register any transfer which does not comply with the provisions of Article 7.1, whether or not it is of fully-paid shares.

8. GENERAL MEETINGS AND RESOLUTIONS

8.1 The directors may call general meetings and, on the requisition of members pursuant to the provisions of the Act, shall forthwith proceed to convene an extraordinary general meeting for a date not later than 4 weeks after receipt of the requisition. Regulation 37 of Table A shall not apply.

8.2 In Regulation 115 in the second sentence "48 hours" shall be deleted and "24 hours" shall be substituted therefor.

8.3 No business shall be transacted at any general meeting unless a quorum is present when the meeting proceeds to business, but the absence of a quorum shall not preclude the nomination, election or choice of a chairman which shall not be treated for this purpose as part of the business of the meeting. Save as otherwise provided by Article 8.4, two members present in person or by proxy and entitled to vote shall be a quorum for all purposes. Regulation 40 of Table A shall not apply.

8.4 If a quorum is not present within fifteen minutes (or such longer time, not exceeding half an hour, as the chairman of the meeting may decide to wait) after the time appointed for the meeting, or if during a meeting a quorum ceases to be present, the meeting shall stand adjourned to such day and at such other time and place as the chairman of the meeting may determine and at such adjourned meeting one member present in person or by proxy (whatever the number of shares held by him) shall be a quorum. It shall not be necessary to give notice of any meeting adjourned through want of a quorum. Regulation 41 of Table A shall not apply.

8.5 If at any General Meeting any votes shall be counted which ought not to have been counted or which might have been rejected, the error shall not vitiate the result of the voting unless it be pointed out at the same meeting, and not in that case unless it shall, in the opinion of the

3

101

chairman of the meeting, be of sufficient magnitude to vitiate the result of the voting. Regulation 58 shall not apply.

9.   PROXIES

An instrument appointing a proxy shall be in writing, executed by or on behalf of the appointor and in any usual or common form or in such other form as the directors may approve and shall be deemed to confer authority to vote on any amendment of a resolution put to the meeting for which it is given as the proxy thinks fit. The instrument of proxy shall, unless the contrary is stated therein, be valid as well for any adjournment of the meeting as for the meeting to which it relates. The instrument appointing a proxy and any authority under which it is executed shall be deposited at the office of the Company, or immediately prior to the commencement of a general meeting or class meeting, with the Secretary or the chairman of that meeting. Regulations 60, 61 and 62 shall not apply.

10.   APPOINTMENT AND RETIREMENT OF DIRECTORS

10.1   The number of the directors shall be two or such greater number as may be determined by ordinary resolution of the Company.

10.2   Subject to Article 10.1, any member or members holding in aggregate a majority in nominal value of such of the issued share capital for the time being of the Company as carries the right of attending and voting at general meetings of the Company, by memorandum in writing signed by or on behalf of him or them and delivered to the office or tendered at a meeting of the directors or at a general meeting of the Company may at any time and from time to time appoint any person to be a director either to fill a vacancy or as an additional director or remove any director from office howsoever appointed. Any such removal from office shall be deemed to be an act of the Company and shall have effect without prejudice to any claim for damages for breach of any contract of service between him and the Company.

10.3   Without prejudice to the powers conferred by Article 10.2, any person may be appointed a director by the directors either to fill a vacancy or as an additional director.

10.4   No director shall be required to retire or vacate his office, and no person shall be ineligible for appointment as a director, by reason of his having attained any particular age.

10.5   Regulations 73 to 80 (inclusive) and the last sentence of Regulation 84 of Table A shall not apply.

11.   DISQUALIFICATION OF DIRECTORS

The office of a director shall be vacated not only upon the happening of any of the events mentioned in Regulation 81 of Table A but also if he is removed from office pursuant to these Articles. Regulation 81 of Table A shall be modified accordingly.

4

12. ALTERNATE DIRECTORS

12.1 Any director (other than an alternate director) may appoint any other director, or any other person who is willing to act, to be an alternate director and may remove from office an alternate director so appointed by him. Regulation 65 of Table A shall not apply.

12.2 A director or any other person may act as alternate director to represent more than one director, and an alternate director shall be entitled at meetings of the directors or any committee of the directors to one vote for every director which he represents in addition to his own vote (if any) as a director, but he shall count as only one for the purpose of determining whether a quorum if present.

12.3 An alternate director shall cease to be an alternate director if his appointor ceases for any reason to be a director. Regulation 67 of Table A shall not apply.

13. POWERS OF DIRECTORS

The directors may, by power of attorney or otherwise, appoint any person to be the agent of the Company upon such terms (including terms as to remuneration) as they may think fit and may delegate to any person so appointed any of the powers vested in or exercisable by them including power to sub-delegate. The directors may remove any person appointed under this Article and may revoke or vary such delegation but no person dealing in good faith and without notice of any such revocation or variation shall be affected by it. Regulation 71 of Table A shall not apply.

14. DELEGATION OF DIRECTORS' POWERS

The directors may delegate any of their powers to committees consisting of such person or persons (whether directors or not) as they think fit. Regulation 72 of Table A shall be modified accordingly.

15. DIRECTORS' GRATUITIES AND PENSIONS

15.1 The directors, on behalf of the Company, may exercise all the powers of the Company to provide benefits, either by the payment of gratuities or pensions or by insurance or in any other manner whether similar to the foregoing or not, for any director or former director or the relations, connections or dependants of any director or former director who holds or has held any executive office or employment with the Company or with any body corporate which is or has been a subsidiary of the Company or with a predecessor in business of the Company or of any such subsidiary and may contribute to any fund and pay premiums for the purchase or provisions of any such benefit. No director or former director shall be accountable to the Company or the members for any benefit provided pursuant to this Article and the receipt of any such benefit shall not disqualify any person from being or becoming a director of the Company. Regulation 87 of Table A shall not apply.

5

15.2 The directors may by resolution exercise any power conferred by the Act to make provision for the benefit of persons employed or formerly employed by the Company or any of its subsidiaries in connection with the cessation or the transfer to any person of the whole or part of the undertaking of the company or that subsidiary.

16. PROCEEDINGS OF DIRECTORS

16.1 A director who to his knowledge is in any way, whether directly or indirectly, interested in a contract or proposed contract (within the meaning of section 317 of the Act) with the Company shall declare the nature of his interest at a meeting of the directors in accordance with that section. Subject where applicable to such disclosure, a director shall be entitled to vote in respect of any such contract or proposed contract in which he is interested and if he shall do so his vote shall be counted and he shall be taken into account in ascertaining whether a quorum is present. Regulations 94 to 96 (inclusive) of Table A shall not apply.

16.2 Without prejudice to the first sentence of Regulation 88 of Table A, a meeting of the directors or of a committee of the directors may consist of a conference between directors who are not all in one place, but of whom each is able (directly or by telephonic communication) to speak to each of the others, and to be heard by each of the others simultaneously; and the word "meeting" in these Articles and in Table A shall be construed accordingly.

17. NOTICES

17.1 Any notice or other document may be served on or delivered to any member by the Company either personally or by sending it by post in a prepaid envelope or wrapper addressed to the member at his registered address, or by leaving it at that address addressed to the member, or by any other means authorised in writing by the member concerned. In the case of joint holders of a share, service or delivery of any notice or other document on or to one of the joint holders shall for all purposes be deemed a sufficient service on or delivery to all the joint holders. Regulation 112 of Table A shall be modified accordingly.

17.2 Any notice or other document, if sent by post, shall be deemed to have been served or delivered on the day following that on which it was put in the post and, in proving such service or delivery, it shall be sufficient to prove that the notice or document was properly addressed, stamped and put in the post. Any notice or other document left at a registered address otherwise than by post shall be deemed to have been served or delivered on the day it was so left. Regulation 115 of Table A shall not apply.

17.3 Any notice or other document may be served on or delivered to any person or persons entitled to a share in consequence of the death or bankruptcy of a member by the Company in any manner which would be permitted by the Articles if the person or persons concerned were a member or were members and either addressed to him or them by name or by the title of representatives of the deceased or trustee of the bankrupt or by any like description at the address (if any) within the United Kingdom supplied by him or them for that purpose. Until such address has been supplied, a notice or other document may be served on or delivered to the

6

104

person or persons so entitled in any manner in which it might have been served or given if the death or bankruptcy had not occurred. Regulation 116 of Table A shall not apply.

18. INDEMNITY

18.1 Subject to the provisions of the Act, but without prejudice to any indemnity to which the person concerned may otherwise be entitled, every director or other officer or auditor of the Company shall be indemnified out of the assets of the Company against any liability incurred by him as such director or other officer or auditor in defending any proceedings, whether civil or criminal, in which judgment is given in his favour or in which he is acquitted or in connection with any application in which relief is granted to him by the court from liability. Regulation 118 of Table A shall not apply.

18.2 The directors shall have power to purchase and maintain for any director, officer or auditor of the Company, insurance against any such liability as is referred to in section 310(1) of the Act.

7

105

NAMES AND ADDRESSES OF SUBSCRIBERS

New Delhi Television Ltd.
W-17, Greater Kailash-I
New Delhi 110048
Delhi
India

for and on behalf of
New Delhi Television Ltd.

NDTV Investments Pvt. Ltd
W-17, Greater Kailash-I
New Delhi 110048
Delhi
India

for and on behalf of
NDTV Investments Pvt. Ltd

Dated this 30 day of November 2006

Witness to the above signature:

Name: Sudhanshu Kumar Singh

Address: D-207, Okha Industrial Estate, Phase-III, New Delhi - 110020

Occupation: Service

8

Companies House
— for the record —

AR01 (ef)

Annual Return

Received for filing in Electronic Format on the: **25/02/2010**   XUGKKHTL

Company Name:	NDTV NETWORKS PLC
Company Number:	06015161
Date of this return:	30/11/2009
SIC codes:	7487
Company Type:	**Public limited company**
Situation of Registered Office:	**SEVENTH FLOOR** **90 HIGH HOLBORN** **LONDON** **WC1V 6XX**

Officers of the company

Service Address:

Electronically Filed Document for Company Number: **06015161**   *Page:* 1

NDTV FRAUDS

Company Secretary *1*

Type:	**Corporate**
Name:	**OLSWANG COSEC LIMITED**
Registered or principal address:	**SEVENTH FLOOR 90 HIGH HOLBORN** **LONDON** **UNITED KINGDOM** **WC1V 6XX**

European Economic Area (EEA) Company

Register Location:	**UNITED KINGDOM**
Registration Number:	**04051235**

Consented to Act: **Y**   *Date authorised:*   *Authenticated:* **ERRO**

Company Director   *1*

Type:	**Person**
Full forename(s):	**ISHWARI PRASAD**
Surname:	**BAJPAI**
Former names:	
Service Address:	**33B FRIENDS COLONY EAST** **NEW DELHI** **110065**

Country/State Usually Resident: **INDIA**

Date of Birth: **23/04/1952**   *Nationality:* **INDIAN**
Occupation: **SERVICE**

Company Director   2

Type:	**Person**
Full forename(s):	**VIKRAMADITYA**
Surname:	**CHANDRA**
Former names:	
Service Address:	**C-4/2, 1ST FLOOR** **VISANT VIHAR** **NEW DELHI** **FOREIGN**

Country/State Usually Resident: **INDIA**

Date of Birth: **07/01/1967**   *Nationality:* **INDIAN**
Occupation: **JOURNALIST**

Company Director   3

Type:	**Person**
Full forename(s):	**SAMEER CHANDRAN**
Surname:	**NAIR**
Former names:	
Service Address:	**F.NO 4S2 & 4S4 3RD FLOOR SAMSHIBA, NARGIS DUTT** **ROAD** **PALLI HILL, BANDRA(W)** **MUMBAI**

Country/State Usually Resident: **INDIA**

Date of Birth: **03/12/1964**   *Nationality:* **INDIAN**
Occupation: **SERVICE**

Company Director   4

Type:	**Person**
Full forename(s):	**JOHN MARTIN**
Surname:	**O LOAN**
Former names:	
Service Address:	**4 ANCASTER HOUSE**
	RICHMOND HILL
	RICHMOND
	SURREY
	TW10 6RN

Country/State Usually Resident: **UNITED KINGDOM**

Date of Birth: **14/12/1948**   *Nationality:* **AUSTRALIAN**

Occupation: **CONSULTANT MEDIA TECHNOLOGY &**

Company Director   5

Type:	**Person**
Full forename(s):	**KEYUR**
Surname:	**PATEL**
Former names:	
Service Address:	**188 MINNA STREET, #23E**
	SAN FRANCISCO
	CALIFORNIA 94103
	FOREIGN

Country/State Usually Resident: **USA**

Date of Birth: **05/05/1965**   *Nationality:* **USA**

Occupation: **DIRECTOR**

Company Director 6

Type:	**Person**
Full forename(s):	**KOTIKALAPUDI VENKATA LAKSHMI NARAYAN**
Surname:	**RAO**
Former names:	
Service Address:	**26 SECOND FLOOR,NRI COMPLEX** **MANDAKINI** **NEW DELHI** **110019**

Country/State Usually Resident: **INDIA**

Date of Birth: **09/04/1954**　　　　*Nationality:* **INDIAN**
Occupation: **SERVICE**

Company Director 7

Type:	**Person**
Full forename(s):	**DR PRANNOY**
Surname:	**ROY**
Former names:	
Service Address:	**B-207, GREATER KAILASH** **NEW DELHI** **110048** **FOREIGN**

Country/State Usually Resident: **INDIA**

Date of Birth: **15/10/1949**　　　　*Nationality:* **INDIAN**
Occupation: **ECONOMIST**

NDTV FRAUDS

Statement of Capital (Share Capital)

Class of shares	A PREFERRED	*Number allotted*	25575
		Aggregate nominal value	2557.5
Currency	GBP	*Amount paid per share*	.1
		Amount unpaid per share	0

Prescribed particulars
EACH A PREFERRED SHARES SHALL CARRY ONE VOTE FOR EACH SHARE OF ORDINARY SHARES INTO WHICH SUCH A PREFERRED SHARES COULD THEN BE CONVERTED INTO. VOTES ON SHARES MAY BE EXERCISED: - ON A SHOW OF HANDS, BY EVERY MEMBER WHO (BEING AN INDIVIDUAL) IS PRESENT IN PERSON OR BY PROXY OR (BEING A CORPORATION) IS PRESENT BY A REPRESENTATIVE OR BY PROXY, NOT BEING HIMSELF A MEMBER (IN WHICH CASE EACH MEMBER HOLDING SHARES SHALL HAVE ONE VOTE); AND - ON A POLL, BY EVERY MEMBER WHO (BEING AN INDIVIDUAL) IS PRESENT IN PERSON OR BY PROXY OR (BEING A CORPORATION) IS PRESENT BY A REPRESENTATIVE OR BY A PROXY (IN WHICH CASE EACH MEMBER HOLDING SHARES SHALL HAVE SUCH NUMBER OF VOTES ATTRIBUTABLE TO THE SHARES SO HELD

Class of shares	CONVERTIBLE REDEEMABLE	*Number allotted*	15650
		Aggregate nominal value	1565
Currency	GBP	*Amount paid per share*	.1
		Amount unpaid per share	0

Prescribed particulars
THE CONVERTIBLE NON-VOTING SHARES CARRY NO RIGHT TO VOTE.

Class of shares	ORDINARY	*Number allotted*	543478
		Aggregate nominal value	54347.8
Currency	GBP	*Amount paid per share*	.1
		Amount unpaid per share	0

Prescribed particulars
EACH ORDINARY SHARE SHALL CARRY ONE VOTE PER SHARE. VOTES ON SHARES MAY BE EXERCISED: ON A SHOW OF HANDS, BY EVERY MEMBER WHO (BEING AN INDIVIDUAL) IS PRESENT IN PERSON OR BY PROXY OR (BEING A CORPORATION) IS PRESENT BY A REPRESENTATIVE OR BY PROXY, NOT BEING HIMSELF A MEMBER (IN WHICH CASE EACH MEMBER HOLDING SHARES SHALL HAVE ONE VOTE); AND ON A POLL, BY EVERY MEMBER WHO (BEING AN INDIVIDUAL) IS PRESENT IN PERSON OR BY PROXY OR (BEING A CORPORATION) IS PRESENT BY A REPRESENTATIVE OR BY A PROXY (IN WHICH CASE EACH MEMBER HOLDING SHARES SHALL HAVE SUCH NUMBER OF VOTES ATTRIBUTABLE TO THE SHARES SO HELD CALCULATED BY REFERENCE TO THE ABOVE).

Statement of Capital (Totals)

Currency	GBP		
		Total number of shares	584703
		Total aggregate nominal value	58470.3

Full Details of Shareholders

The details below relate to individuals / corporate bodies that were shareholders as at 30/11/2009 or that had ceased to be shareholders since the made up date of the previous Annual Return

A full list of shareholders for a private or non-traded public company are shown below

Shareholding : 1

25575 A PREFERRED Shares held as at 30/11/2009

Name: **FUSE & MEDIA HOLDINGS LP**

Address:

Shareholding : 2

978 CONVERTIBLE REDEEMABLE Shares held as at 30/11/2009

Name: **ISHWARI PRASAD BAJPAI**

Address:

NDTV FRAUDS

Shareholding : 3	
	2717 ORDINARY Shares held as at 30/11/2009
Name:	ISHWARI PRASAD BAJPAI
Address:	

Shareholding : 4	
	782 CONVERTIBLE REDEEMABLE Shares held as at 30/11/2009
Name:	SAURAV BANERJEE
Address:	

Shareholding : 5	
	2174 ORDINARY Shares held as at 30/11/2009
Name:	SAURAV BANERJEE
Address:	

Shareholding : 6

1956 CONVERTIBLE REDEEMABLE Shares held as at 30/11/2009

Name: SMEETA CHAKRABARTI

Address:

Shareholding : 7

5435 ORDINARY Shares held as at 30/11/2009

Name: SMEETA CHAKRABARTI

Address:

Shareholding : 8

2543 CONVERTIBLE REDEEMABLE Shares held as at 30/11/2009

Name: VIKRAMADITYA CHANDRA

Address:

NDTV FRAUDS

Shareholding : 9

7065 ORDINARY Shares held as at 30/11/2009

Name: **VIKRAMADITYA CHANDRA**

Address:

Shareholding : 10

978 CONVERTIBLE REDEEMABLE Shares held as at 30/11/2009

Name: **BARKHA DUTT**

Address:

Shareholding : 11

2717 ORDINARY Shares held as at 30/11/2009

Name: **BARKHA DUTT**

Address:

Shareholding   : *12*
2446 CONVERTIBLE REDEEMABLE Shares held as at 30/11/2009

Name: **SANJAY DUTT**

Address:

Shareholding   : *13*
6793 ORDINARY Shares held as at 30/11/2009

Name: **SANJAY DUTT**

Address:

Shareholding   : *14*
782 CONVERTIBLE REDEEMABLE Shares held as at 30/11/2009

Name: **RAJIV MATHUR**

Address:

NDTV FRAUDS

Shareholding : 15

2174 ORDINARY Shares held as at 30/11/2009

Name: **RAJIV MATHUR**

Address:

Shareholding : 16

4598 CONVERTIBLE REDEEMABLE Shares held as at 30/11/2009

Name: **KOTIKALAPUDI VENKATA LAKSMI NARAYAN RAO**

Address:

Shareholding : 17

12773 ORDINARY Shares held as at 30/11/2009

Name: **KOTIKALAPUDI VENKATA LAKSMI NARAYAN RAO**

Address:

Shareholding   : 18
   196 CONVERTIBLE REDEEMABLE Shares held as at 30/11/2009

Name: SHYATTO RAHA

Address:

Shareholding   : 19
   543 ORDINARY Shares held as at 30/11/2009

Name: SHYATTO RAHA

Address:

Shareholding   : 20
   391 CONVERTIBLE REDEEMABLE Shares held as at 30/11/2009

Name: SUPARNA SINGH

Address:

Shareholding : *21*

1087 ORDINARY Shares held as at 30/11/2009

Name: SUPARNA SINGH

Address:

Shareholding : *22*

1 ORDINARY Shares held as at 30/11/2009

Name: NDTV INVESTMENTS PVT. LTD.

Address:

Shareholding : *23*

499998 ORDINARY Shares held as at 30/11/2009

Name: NDTV BV

Address:

Shareholding   : 24

1 ORDINARY Shares held as at 30/11/2009

Name: **NEW DELHI TELEVISION LTD**

Address:

Authorisation

Authenticated

This form was authorised by one of the following:

Director, Secretary, Person Authorised, Charity Commission Receiver and Manager, CIC Manager, Judicial Factor.

Annex 3: Swamy's complaint to the Prime Minister

DR. SUBRAMANIAN SWAMY Ph.D. (Harvard)
Cabinet Minister for Commerce, Law & Justice (1990-91)
Chairman (with Cabinet rank), Commission on Labour
Standards and International Trade (1994-96)
Former Professor of Economics, Indian Institute of
Technology, Delhi & Faculty, Harvard University

MEMBER OF PARLIAMENT (Rajya Sabha)
Res.: AB-14, Pandara Road, New Delhi - 110 003
Phone & Fax : +91 11 23387278
E-mail : swamy39@gmail.com
swamy@post.harvard.edu

प्रधान मंत्री कार्यालय
Prime Minister's Office
डाक अनुभाग
DAK SECTION
Date 10|8|16

August 10, 2016

Dear Prime Minister:

Re : (1) CBI should register a case against NDTV under Prevention of Corruption Act in Aircel-Maxis case for routing 50 million dollars from Astro All Asia Network.

(2) Enforcement Directorate (ED) registration of a case against NDTV under PMLA for Rs.2030 crore and Rs.640 crore money laundering.

CBI is not doing its statutory duty following the Enforcement Directorate's finding of NDTV's money laundering of 50 million US dollars in the Aircel Maxis scam chargesheet.

According to ED's chargesheet and LR sent by the 2G Court to UK, the NDTV has received $50 million from Maxis subsidiary Astro- All Asia Network during the scam during the period. Incidentally Astro AAN is also already charged as accused by CBI and ED for providing bribe to Sun TV.

The ED in its chargesheet filed before 2G Court said that during the same period in 2007, NDTV also received $50 million from Astro AAN and it is and prima facie proceeds of illegal activity in Aircel-Maxis scam. Therefore CBI statutorily under the Prevention of Corruption Act is bound to act on this issue of money transfer to NDTV.

The TV channel's top people should be therefore questioned initially by the CBI to find on whose behest the money came to them in Aircel-Maxis deal, which deal was prima facie illegally approved by former Finance Minister P Chidambaram for the benefit of his son Karthi Chidambaram through the latter's company Advantage Strategic Consultants Company .

—2—

Enforcement Directorate had earlier initiated proceeding against NDTV for FEMA violations and having determined illegality slapped fine of Rs. 2030 crore. The case is in the arbitration stage and RBI under Governor Raghuram Rajan had tried to save NDTV through paying meagre fine. These FEMA violations are charged for siphoning and laundering of illicit money by floating a subsidiary in London.

The Directors of the London company known as NDTV Networks Plc (NNPLC) are Prannoy Roy, Radhika Roy, Barkha Dutt, Vikram Chandra, Sonia Singh and Suparna Singh.

Enforcement Directorate has not yet summoned these key players involved in the huge money laundering and sham transactions. Annual Return filed by NNPLC to UK's Company Registry in Dec 2010 shows that these persons were active Directors (Details of the documents filed by NNPLC in UK's Company Registry, if needed, may be applied from UK's Company House)

Mr. P Chidambaram's loyal appointees in the Finance Ministry made when he was FM, are now actively trying to dilute the gravity by registering the cases under FEMA to bypass criminality and providing an escape route of paying fines only.

This however is a clear criminal case of money laundering and the case should be registered under PMLA, and ED should be permitted to call all the high profile operators of NDTV who have been taking the cover being journalists with political patronage, to suppress the criminal investiagtion.

NDTV is also having a secret company in Cayman Island for money laundering. The company's name is : Fuse & Media Holdings LP. Address is : Walker House, 87 Mary Street, George Town, Grand Cayman, Cayman Islands. This secret company is also a shareholder of NNPLC in London.

Recently, Income Tax [F.No. DCIT/Circel-18(1) 2016-17 dtd June 15, 2016] has found evasion of Rs.640 crore money received by NDTV and therefore were slapped with a fine of Rs.525 crore.

—3—

This is also a case of obvious money laundering of Rs.640 crore [through Bermuda, facilitated by P. Chidambaram in March 2008 as the Minister in charge, should also be converted to a PMLA case to bring to public knowledge the identity of persons of NDTV abetting or committing these financial crimes. ED be permitted to register another PMLA case for this offence.

With Regards   Yours truly

Subramanian Swamy

123

Annex 4: Income Tax notice slapping Rs. 525 crores fine

Office of the
Deputy Commissioner of Income Tax
Circle-18(1), Room No. 212, C.R. Building
I. P. Estate, New Delhi- 110002

F.No. DCIT/Circle-18(1)/2016-17/_____   Dated : 1...

To

    The Principal Officer,
    M/s. New Delhi Television Limited,
    207, Okhla Industrial Estate, Phase-III,
    New Delhi – 110 020.

Sir,

    Sub : Show cause notice regarding imposition of penalty u/s 271(1)(c) of the Act
    in the case of M/s. New Delhi Television Limited for AY 2009-1...
    Regarding –

Please refer to the above subject.

2.   The draft order u/s 144C(1) of the Income Tax Act, 1961 (the "**Act**") in your case for AY 2009-10 was passed on 31.03.2013 and your income was proposed to be assessed at Rs. 641,08,11,990/- as against loss of Rs. 64,83,91,422/- as declared by you in your return of income. Additions totalling Rs. 705,92,03,412/- were proposed in the draft order.

Findings during the assessment proceedings

3.   Against the proposed additions, M/s. New Delhi Television Limited ("NDTV" the "assessee company") filed objections before the Dispute Resolution Panel ("DRP"), which issued directions u/s 144C(5) of the Act on 31.12.2013 and confirmed additions amounting to Rs. 648,42,28,619/- as proposed in the draft order and further enhanced your taxable income by another Rs. 254,75,00,000/-.

4.   In compliance with the directions, the final assessment order was passed u/s 144/144C(13) on 21.02.2014 at an income of Rs. 838,33,37,197/-, wherein the following additions totaling Rs. 903,17,28,619/- were made :-

(in INR)

S. No.	Nature of addition	Amount of addition
1	Disallowance u/s 14A	78,40,990
2	Transfer Pricing adjustments	5,09,65,629
3	Addition u/s 69A on account of unexplained money	642,54,22,000
4	Addition u/s 68 on account of unexplained unsecured loans	254,75,00,000
	Total	903,17,28,619

-Show cause notice in the case of M/s. New Delhi Television Limited for AY 2009-10-

5.   Penalty proceedings u/s 271(1)(c) of the Act were simultaneously initiated and notice u/s 274 read with section 271(1)(c) of the Act was issued to you on 21.02.2014. However, no reply has been received from you on the merits of the case till date.

6.   The facts of the case regarding the addition of Rs. 642,54,22,000/- are that during the year under consideration, New Delhi Television Ltd. (NDTV), along with four of its subsidiaries namely NDTV BV, NDTV Networks BV (NNBV), NDTV Networks International Holdings BV (NNIH) and NDTV Networks Plc (NNPLC), had entered into an agreement dated 23.05.2008 with NBC Universal Inc. (NBC) and Universal Studios International BV (USBV). As a result, an amount of Rs. 642,54,22,000/- (US $150 million) was received during the year by NNIH. The amount was received on account of subscription of 915,498 shares into NDTV Networks International Holdings BV equivalent to 26% effective indirect stake in NDTV Networks Plc.

7.   It is further noticed that taking into account the consideration of Rs. 642,54,22,000/- for 915,498 shares, the sale value per share thus comes to Rs. 7,015.05 per share. The face value of share of NNIH at the relevant time was around $ 1 per share, i.e. equivalent to Rs. 45/- to Rs. 50/- per share approx.

8.   The above sale value was despite the fact that neither NNIH nor NNPLC were having any business activities. NNIH was a holding company and NNPLC was incorporated to promote the interests of NNIH and other group companies. NNPLC did not have any business activities. It had no fixed assets and there was no rent paid. NNPLC did not even have any employee in UK and the only employee in NNPLC was Mr. Vikramaditya Chandra, who was designated as CEO of this company. However, Mr. Chandra was also based in India only. Apart from incorporation in UK, NNPLC had no presence in UK. The address of NNPLC in UK was that of the Company Secretary dealing with its tax matters. Most of the Directors of NNPLC were Indians and the audit report of NNPLC was signed at Gurgaon in India. The authorized share capital of NNPLC was only about Rs. 47 lacs. NNPLC had declared loss of Rs. 8.67 crores for the year ending 31.03.2009. The subscription of a share of the value around Rs. 50/- per share by USBV was @ Rs. 7,015/- per share, i.e. 140 times of the face value.

9.   It is also pertinent to record that **before purchasing the subscription, NBCU did not even obtain any independent valuation from a third party**. Vide reply dated 30.03.2013, NDTV has admitted and confirmed that no independent valuation report for determining the value of shares of NNIH was obtained. The subscription price is stated to be "*a negotiated price arrived between the parties based on proposed business potential and business forecast and projections*". Since no prudent businessman will purchase the shares of a paper company at a price, which was more than 140 times of the face value without any credible valuation, the transaction was held as a part of scheme of routing own fund of the assessee company in the assessment order.

NDTV FRAUDS

10. It was observed during the assessment proceedings that subsequently, during the immediately succeeding FY 2009-10, the very same shares were bought back by NDTV BV for Rs. 58.08 crores @ Rs. 634.17 per share. If the transactions were not sham, how could the same shares having face value of Rs. 50/- per share approx. be issued @ Rs. 7015.05 per share and further bought back @ Rs. 634.17 per share. That also is claimed in a situation when the issue of shares and the repurchase of shares are by an entity and its immediate subsidiary respectively. The transaction resulted in a claim of loss amounting to Rs. 584.45 crores for USBV and simultaneously resulted in an introduction of undisclosed income of Rs. 642.54 crores in the books of accounts of the NDTV group. As already recorded, no independent valuation was ever carried out by the group companies or by the USBV and the issue rate as well as the repurchase rate are claimed to be solely based on estimates and business projections. It is pertinent to mention that although the agreement dated 23.05.2008 stipulated a 5 Year Business Plan, which involved annual review and the 1st annual review was scheduled to be carried out before the end of financial year 2009-10 on 31.03.2010. However, even before the 1st annual review could take place, the shares were allegedly bought back by NDTV Networks BV without any review of progress of business plan and without any valuation carried out by either party. These facts made it evident during the assessment proceedings that the transaction was not genuine.

11. The whole transaction thus had no commercial purpose or economic substance and its purpose was merely to evade tax and to constitute sham, colorable or bogus transactions with the pretense of corporate and commercial trading and in such circumstances, the corporate veil was therefore pierced while making the assessment of the assessee company. Once the corporate veil was lifted in the context of the impugned transaction in the present case, the clear facts emerging regarding the transaction revealed that the transaction was engineered to result in claim of loss to USBV and corresponding routing of the assessee's own undisclosed money through its subsidiary. This finding has been confirmed by the DRP.

12. While confirming the above findings, the DRP has specifically observed that the impugned transaction was sham and engineered to bring unexplained money of Rs. 642.54 crore by way of routing through a complex corporate structure, which lacked any commercial substance. The observations of the DRP in this regard are reproduced below :

> "5.16 DRP has carefully considered the entire gamut of transaction and is of the opinion that the structure of holding/ subsidiary companies and the transaction as narrated above, without any commercial substance, do warrant lifting the corporate veil to identify the true nature of the transaction. Though AO in his remand report has said that the money has not been recorded in the books of assessee, after lifting the corporate veil, the DRP finds that in this case a sum of Rs. 642,54,22,000/- has been found credited in the books of assessee/ its subsidiary for the previous year (FY 2008-09) under consideration. Though the assessee has sought to explain the above amount through the lengthy and circuitous transactions, the commercial substance/ economic rationale for such transaction has not

-Show cause notice in the case of M/s. New Delhi Television Limited for AY 2009-10-

been satisfactorily explained. Assessee's theory of having sold a "Dream" to the investor has not been substantiated by any credible evidence as no details have been filed whatsoever for the so called business projections and the basis for computation of the sale price of the share at the astronomical price of Rs. 7,015/- which is 159 times of its face value of Rs. 45/-. Needless to mention that the subject company whose shares were sold was incurring huge losses and there was hardly any worthwhile business to justify the above sale price. Interestingly, the assessee/ subsidiaries have again repurchased the same share in the very next financial year at the price of Rs. 634.17 per share totalling Rs. 58 crores. Here also no details/ justification has been given by the assessee as to how the above buy back price was fixed by the assessee when the so called "Dream" went bust, as being claimed by assessee. What was the justification for the assessee to buy back the shares of nearly defunct and own subsidiary company at a value which was more than 12 times of the face value. **The totality of the transaction clearly lead to the inescapable conclusion that the entire transaction of sale & subsequent buy back of shares was a "sham" transaction entered into by the assessee with the sole motive of introducing Rs. 642,54,22,000/- in its books and providing loss of Rs. 584.46 crores to Universal Studios BV Netherlands.**

5.16.1. In view of the facts and finding as mentioned above and taking the totality of the picture into consideration, **it is held that assessee has brought an amount of Rs. 642,54,22,000/- being unexplained money in to its books through its subsidiary NDTV Networks BV Netherlands. It is pertinent to** mention that, as per the admission of the assessee **the above subsidiary has been subsequently liquidated, which shows that the same was floated only to create a front for introducing the above amount."**

[Emphasis supplied]

13.   From the above, it is evident that there is a finding arrived at in the assessment order regarding creation of a façade in the nature of complex corporate structure and routing of money through sham transactions using this structure and this finding has been confirmed by the DRP as narrated above.

Findings during the course of penalty proceedings

14.   Copy of agreement dated 23.05.2008 filed during the course of assessment proceedings was not reliable evidence

14.1   During the assessment proceedings for AY 2009-10, the assessee company filed copy of agreement dated 23.05.2008 in respect of alleged transaction of subscription by USBV in the shares of NNIH, however, this document had no evidentiary value. It was a photo copy, which was neither apostle certified nor was signed by any of the parties on each page nor it

Page 4 of 14

127

-Show cause notice in the case of M/s. New Delhi Television Limited for AY 2009-10-

was signed by all the parties even on the same page. Further, the impugned agreement was not even signed by CA Holding CV, Bermuda, which was the actual parent company of USBV. Even the terms and conditions of the agreement were not complied with, because the agreement dated 23.05.2008 stipulated a 5 Year Business Plan, which involved annual review and the 1st annual review was scheduled to be carried out before the end of financial year 2009-10 on 31.03.2010. However, even before the 1st annual review could take place, the shares were allegedly bought back by NDTV Networks BV without any review of progress of business plan and without any valuation carried out by either party. The celerity with which the shares were bought back without waiting for even the 1st review makes it evident that the agreement was not genuine and there was no intention to comply with the said agreement.

15. **Parent company of USBV is in Bermuda and not in USA**

15.1 It is pertinent to mention that NDTV had represented throughout before the AO, the DRP and the ITAT that NBC Universal Inc., USA ("NBCU") is the parent company of Universal Studios International BV ("USBV"), which invested US $ 150 million (INR 642,54,22,000) in subscription of shares of NDTV Networks International Holdings BV ("NNIH"). However, this is found to be factually incorrect. The correct position is that 100% of shares of USBV were held by NBCU Dutch Holding (Bermuda) Limited, which was holding them in its capacity as General Managing Partner of CA Holding CV, Bermuda. It is pertinent to point out that the parent company in Bermuda was not even a party to the agreement for subscription of shares of NNIH by USBV.

15.2 Perusal of Annual Report of Universal Studios International BV for the year 2008 reveals that the parent company of USBV is NBCU Dutch Holding (Bermuda) Limited, which is holding the shares of USBV acting in its capacity as General Managing Partner of CA Holding CV Bermuda. The Annual Report mentions as under :-

"The authorised share capital amounts to EUR 2,268,900 (2007: EUR 2,268,900) and consists of 5,000 shares (2007: 5,000 shares) of EUR 453.78 each.

The issued and fully paid share capital comprises 2,680 shares (2007: 2,680 shares) of EUR 453.78 each and has been translated into USD at the year-end exchange rate (December 31,2008: EUR 1 = 1.35240; December 31,2007: EUR 1 = USD 1.447890).

All shares are held by NBCU Dutch Holding (Bermuda) Limited acting in its capacity as General Managing Partner of CA Holding CV, Bermuda."

[Emphasis supplied]

-Show cause notice in the case of M/s. New Delhi Television Limited for AY 2009-10-

16. Money introduced as share application money and securities premium transferred to NDTV in the form of dividend

16.1 NNIH was also a shell company 100% owned by NDTV. It had no assets, employee, business or commercial activities. The only asset was the direct ownership of shell company NDTV Networks BV and indirect ownership of another shell company NNPLC. The entire capital of NNIH was a mere Rs. 12 lacs invested by NDTV. Inspite of this, NNIH was able to issue fresh shares of the value of Rs. 6 lacs and was able to sell those **fresh shares of Rs. 6 lacs value at an astronomical share premium of Rs. 642.48 crores received from USBV, the subsidiary of an entity based in tax haven jurisdiction Bermuda.** In another surprise move, **immediately after receipt of money ostensibly in lieu of fresh shares, NNIH declared dividend out of its securities premium account terming it as 'freely distributable reserves' and distributed dividend amounting to Rs. 643.35 crore to NDTV Networks BV, which was 68.60% shareholder, whereas no dividend was distributed to USBV, which was 31.40% shareholder** and which had brought the entire money of Rs. 642.54 crore into NNIH.

16.2 In this regard, it is pertinent to mention that the statement of Mr. KVL Narayan Rao, Director of the assessee company and the then Group CEO, was recorded on oath u/s 131 of the Act on 23.07.2015, copy of which is enclosed. In this statement, in response to question no. 3, when asked about the rationale of incorporation of plethora of foreign subsidiaries, he admitted that the foreign subsidiaries were incorporated to circumvent the restriction imposed by Indian regulations, which confined the foreign direct investment in news channel companies to a maximum of 26%. No other rationale could be provided by him for creation of these many foreign subsidiaries, all like NNPLC without any commercial activities and without any employee or assets, except stating that it was on the advice of experts and for efficiencies. The explanation given by Mr. Rao regarding the objective of defeating the bar of 26% in news channels is not plausible, because the terms of agreement and subsequent events reveal that the fund of USD 150 million was introduced in companies connected with entertainment channels and no fund was introduced in any news channel company. Now if the fund was to be introduced in non-news companies only (like NDTV Imagine Limited, in which 100% FDI was permissible), then there was no bar in bringing the fund directly through FDI into India. This shows the inherent fallacy of the argument raised by Mr. Rao and also exhibits the lack of any commercial purpose or economic substance behind creation of cobweb of foreign subsidiaries. Even otherwise, regulations restricting FDI cannot be flouted by taking recourse to a well-planned scheme for both routing of money and circumventing the FDI regulations. It is a settled proposition of law that what cannot be done directly, is not permissible to be done obliquely, meaning thereby, whatever is prohibited by law to be done, cannot legally be effected by an indirect and circuitous contrivance.

NDTV FRAUDS

16.3   Further, Mr. Rao also admitted in replies to question no. 13, 15 and 16 that no valuation was ever carried out in respect of value of shares of NNIH, neither at the time of alleged subscription by UCBV nor at the time of buyback by NDTV Networks BV. The alleged purpose of the impugned transaction of introduction of funds of USD 150 million by USBV in NNIH was stated to be acquisition of effective indirect stake of 26% in NNPLC. As discussed in para 8 above, NNPLC was a paper company having no worth. In his statement, Mr. Rao fairly admitted in response to question no. 13 that NNPLC got a value of USD 400 million, when ComVentures (now Fuse+ Capital) invested USD 20 million for 5% stake in NNPLC. It is thus clear that even the value ascribed to NNPLC was not based on any real worth, rather, it was a mathematical value, and the transaction of infusion of USD 20 million in NNPLC was an instrument for creating such artificial value. By infusion of USD 20 million corresponding to 5% of shares of NNPLC, mathematically taking the multiplier of 20, the value of NNPLC was artificially put at USD 400 million, apparently in order to make a ground for larger infusion of funds, as actually happened subsequently. However, this does not go to create the actual value in NNPLC. This has already been so held in the TPO's order and the reassessment order for AY 2007-08.

16.4   It is pertinent to mention that during the penalty proceedings, statement of Mr. Sanjay Dutt, Director, M/s. Quantum Securities Private Limited was recorded on oath u/s 131 of the Act on 09.07.2015. Copy of his statement is enclosed. Mr. Sanjay Dutt is the person, who along with Mr. Sanjay Jain was hired as Financial Consultants/Advisors for the impugned corporate structuring. His credibility is established from his statement that he had family relations with Dr. Prannoy Roy and Mrs. Radhika Roy for over 30 years and he studied with Mr. Vikramaditya Chandra, Group CEO in Doon School during the period 1977-1980 and he along with his family and associate companies held shares of NDTV ranging from 100 to 17,00,000 in number at various times and in FY 2006-07, such shareholding was of the value of more than Rs. 70 crore and that he was approached by Dr. Prannoy Roy for the task of corporate structuring. He also stated that he was part of core group led by Mr. Vikram Chandra, in active consultation with PWC and KPMG, which also included the Roys and Mr. Rao and this group was referred to as 'Nines'.

16.5   Mr. Dutt has stated that he along with Mr. Sanjay Jain quit when he became aware that the real purpose was to route the money without any intention of paying taxes and in violation of the various legal provisions. In support of his averments, he has also furnished copies of emails, as described in his statement also, which are reproduced below :-

(i)   Mail dated 21.05.2008 at 10:16 PM from Mr. Vivek Mehra (PWC) to Dr. Prannoy Roy & others :

"Subject: Press Announcements etc

Dear Prannoy and all above

Now that we are reaching the conclusion I wanted to remind everybody that all press releases.. stock exchange releases etc etc both by NDTV and NBCU should be whetted by us

130

-Show cause notice in the case of M/s. New Delhi Television Limited for AY 2009-10-

We must ensure that what is stated is that NBCU is subscribing to shares for a sum of $ 150 m in NDTV Networks group company Overseas for an effective 26 percent stake. **We must not mention that NDTV is receiving the 150 m as dividend or otherwise.**

If asked a question what will the money be used for ??? We need to decide how to answer this question carefully .

Thanks Vivek"

(ii)   Mail dated 22.05.2008 at 02:09 AM from Dr. Prannoy Roy to Mr. Vivek Mehra (PWC) & others :

"Subject: Re: Press Announcements etc

For everyone ...This is very important ...

Could we please have a draft press release Vivek ... Which we can use and send to nbcu. ...

If possible, it's important that the press release should make clear that the money comes in to NDTV and does not stay in Networks"

(iii)   Mail dated 22.05.2008 at 07:58 AM from Mr. Vivek Mehra (PWC) to Dr. Prannoy Roy & others :

"Subject: Re: Press Announcements etc

Prannoy...

I need to start with a base case draft ...can somebody give that to me..

Your second requirement is something I would avoid saying....let's discuss after I have seen a base draft

BR Vivek"

(iv)   Mail dated 22.05.2008 at 02:14 PM from Dr. Prannoy Roy to Mr. Vivek Mehra (PWC) & others :

"Subject FW: Press Announcements etc

Dear Vivek ... Need your final version on this please ... It will be released in a few hours and will need to be cleared by NBCU before that...

The problem we have it that in the last communication we created a real mess:

Thx
Prannoy

NDTV FRAUDS

Dear Vivek ... Here's a first bash

NDTV and NBCU successfully closed their strategic partnership in the NDTV subsidiary NDTV Networks.

For a consideration of US $150 million, NBCU now has an indirect and effective stake of 26 % in NDTV Networks PLC. This effective 26 % stake is held through a proportionate stake in the holding company of NDTV Networks PLC

NBCU has the option in three years to increase their stake in the Networks PLC's holding company to 50%. The NBCU option to increase their stake will be at FMV (Fair Market Value) at the time the option is exercised.

It has been agreed that management control will always remain with NDTV Ltd.

As a consequence of this successful closing of the partnership with NBCU, the parent company NDTV Ltd now has funds of US $150 which gives it the flexibility to use for any opportunities in the future including acquisitions, expansion in the news space, or in the beyond-news space as and when they arise.

The NDTV - NBCU strategic, partnership in the Networks businesses is a coming together of two leading professional media organizations with similar ethics and goals and promises to be a major force in the media scene in India."

(v)   Mail dated 22.05.2008 at 03:06 PM from Mr. Vivek Mehra (PWC) to Dr. Prannoy Roy & others :

"Subject: Re: FW: Press Announcements etc

Dear Prannoy,

Here is a shot at it, based on your draft Appreciate your problems but **honestly the problem could become worse if we give a handle to the tax authorities.** I am concurrently discussing with other partners now the draft below. Let's get on a call ASAP,

Regards
Vivek"

(vi)   Mail dated 22.05.2008 at 03:43 PM from Dr. Prannoy Roy to Mr. Vivek Mehra (PWC) & others :

"Subject: Press Announcements — Final ?

Thanks very much Vivek ... based on our discussion over the telephone, I just wanted to confirm that this is what you have suggested as the final version:

NDTV group and NBCU group have successfully concluded their strategic partnership initiative for the NDTV Networks business.

-Show cause notice in the case of M/s. New Delhi Television Limited for AY 2009-10-

By a subscription of shares for US $150 million, NBCU group now has an effective indirect stake of 26 % in NDTV Networks PLC UK

NBCU has the option in three years to increase their stake, at the then fair market value, in the holding company of Networks PLC to 50% with NDTV group holding an equal 50% stake. Management control will always remain with NDTV group.

As a consequence of this successful closing of the partnership with NBCU group, the parent company NDTV Ltd and it's wholly owned subsidiaries now have access to funds of US $150 mn which gives it the flexibility to use for any opportunities in the future including acquisitions, expansion in the news space, or in the beyond-news space as and when they arise."

(vii) Mail dated 22.05.2008 at 05:30 PM from Mrs. Radhika Roy to Mr. KVL Narayan Rao, Dr. Prannoy Roy & others :

"Subject: RE: Press Announcements - Final ? Dear Narayan,

But this doesn't really address prannoy's concerns arising from our earlier communication and it would be a pity to miss this opportunity to correct any misconceptions. Just to remind you prannoy's four points below:

"1. Everyone thought the money was to be put into Networks ... As a result we got no shareholder value for the Rs 600 crs in NDTV

2. It's very important to state that the money is not in Networks ...But in NDTV ... As this affects the valuation analysts give to the deal... And it's a big boost if they know it's not in Networks and it is in NDTV ... **I know we can't say stake sale (which it is not anyway)... But we do need to clarify that the money is not in Networks**"

[Emphasis supplied]

16.6 From the above, it is evident that even on 22.05.2008, i.e. a day in advance of the date of alleged agreement, it was clear to all that the money introduced through USBV was not at all an investment to be made by USBV, rather, it was a façade created to introduce the money amounting to Rs. 600 crore in NDTV by showing it as investment, immediately converting it to dividend, distributing dividend to NDTV subsidiary only to the exclusion of the other shareholder and then to route it in a circuitous manner through a cobweb of foreign subsidiaries till it finally reached NDTV. The valuation for the subsequent buyback by NDTV group for Rs. 58 crore in October, 2009 was also evidently based on an adjusted figure of Rs. 42.54 crore (received over and above Rs. 600 crore) after giving the effect of forex fluctuation, etc.

16.7 Thus, the real nature of transaction was actively and deliberately concealed under a thorough, methodical and calculated planned strategy.

NDTV FRAUDS

17. **Money is routed back into NDTV through complex cobweb of sham subsidiaries abroad**

17.1 Pursuant to INR 643.35 crore transferred by NNIH to NDTV Networks BV in the form of dividend, NDTV Networks BV further transferred money as under :-

Trail 1

- Out of Rs. 643.35 crore received, NDTV Networks BV invested INR 389 crore in NDTV (Mauritius) Media Limited, a 100% subsidiary of NDTV

- NDTV (Mauritius) Media Limited invested Rs. 387.59 crore in NDTV Studios Limited on 29.09.2008 [*NDTV (Mauritius) Media Limited merged in NDTV One Holdings Limited, Mauritius on 30.09.2011*]

- NDTV Studios Limited merged in NDTV w.e.f. 01.04.2010

Trail 2

- Out of Rs. 643.35 crore received, NDTV Networks BV advanced INR 254.75 crore as unsecured loan to NDTV Networks Plc, UK ("NNPLC")

- NNPLC was liquidated and merged in NDTV One Holdings Limited on 30.09.2011

- NDTV One Holdings Limited merged in NDTV on 02.11.2012

Conscious, deliberate and well planned attempt to conceal particulars of income

18. From the above, it is evident that the funds amounting to USD 150 million, which was the assessee company's own unexplained money, were introduced in NNIH through USBV under a pre-meditated and well planned strategy, taking all factors into account so that the real transaction is not detected by the tax authorities. The mail dated 21.05.2008 written by Mr. Vivek Mehra (PWC) to Dr. Prannoy Roy is an unambiguous advice to Dr. Roy to conceal the true import of the transaction and not to mention that NDTV was receiving the 150 million as dividend or otherwise. It is interesting to observe that even before the inception of shareholding of USBV in NNIH on 23.05.2008, the payment of dividend exclusively to NDTV was fixed. Another mail dated 22.05.2008 written by Mr. Vivek Mehra (PWC) to Dr. Prannoy Roy honestly cautions Dr. Roy that the problem could become worse if NDTV gave a handle to the tax authorities.

-Show cause notice in the case of M/s. New Delhi Television Limited for AY 2009-10-

18.1   It is pertinent to mention that all agreements, whether pertaining to alleged subscription of stake by USBV in NNIH or alleged buyback by NDTV Networks BV, are invariably signed by NDTV itself. As the other companies signing the agreement are mere paper companies and only the assessee company is a real company, therefore, it is clear that the actual party is the assessee company only and the paper companies are only namesakes.

18.2   This proves it beyond doubt that the transaction, which was a colorable device as explained by the Hon'ble Supreme Court in the case of McDowell & Co. Ltd. V. CTO [154 ITR 148 (SC)], was a conscious, deliberate and pre-meditated attempt aimed at tax evasion to conceal the assessee company's own unexplained income. The assessee company was always aware of the untrue façade to be created through this sham transaction and was also aware that the true facts could be discovered by the tax authorities. Being so aware, the assessee company deliberately and under the expert advice of PWC chose to conceal the true facts.

19.   **Facts concealed by the assessee**

19.1   It is observed that the assessee company has concealed the following facts :-

(i)   It has been concealed that the parent company of USBV was **CA Holding CV Bermuda**. There is not even a single reference to the Bermuda parent in the impugned agreement dated 23.05.2008 entered into between the complete chain of parent and all intervening subsidiaries on the one hand and NBCU and USBV on the other hand.

(ii)   It has been concealed that immediately after introduction of money amounting to Rs. 642.54 crore in NNIH, NNIH declared and paid dividend of Rs. 643.35 crore and this dividend was entirely paid to NDTV Networks BV, in exclusion of the other shareholder USBV, which had brought in the entire money of Rs. 642.54 crore as share premium. Instead, the assessee company created a façade of investment by USBV though knowing fully well that money was to be introduced in the form of dividend exclusive to NDTV group.

(iii)   It has been concealed that the actual ownership and control over the money amounting to Rs. 642,54,22,000/- was always with the assessee company only, which introduced this money by creating complex cobweb of sham subsidiaries in Netherlands and UK and later routed this money through sham subsidiaries in Mauritius until the money was ultimately ploughed back into the assessee company in India.

(iv)   It is observed that not only during the assessment proceedings but in the present penalty proceedings also, the assessee company has continued to conceal the true facts. This is apparent from the statement of Mr. KVL Narayan Rao, Director as discussed in para 16.2 above, wherein Mr. Rao has given the rationale for creation of foreign subsidiaries as being the restriction imposed in FDI in news channel companies, whereas actually the funds introduced through foreign subsidiaries were meant for non-news companies only, which could be accomplished through obtaining direct FDI into these companies in India.

19.2 Furnishing of inaccurate particulars by the assessee

(i) The assessee company has furnished documents, which had no evidentiary value, because the agreement dated 23.05.2008 is not signed by all the parties on the same page, the copy of agreement given is not apostle certified and the Bermuda parent of USBV is not even a party to this agreement.

20. Conclusion

20.1 In view of the above facts and circumstances of the case, which involve active, deliberate and planned concealment and misrepresentation of facts, this is a fit case, which merit levy of penalty @ 200% of the tax sought to be evaded. Accordingly, you are requested to show cause as to why penalty u/s 271(1)(c) of the Act read with **Explanation 1** thereof **may not be imposed upon the company for concealment of the particulars of its income in respect of the impugned addition of Rs. 642,54,22,000/-.**

20.2 Similarly, regarding the other three additions as mentioned in para 4 above, you are requested to show cause as to why penalty u/s 271(1)(c) of the Act read with **Explanation 1 thereof @ 100% may not be imposed upon the company for concealment of the particulars of its income in respect of these additions.**

21. Quantum of penalty

21.1 In accordance with the above, the quantum of proposed penalty in the case of the assessee company will be as under :-

Penalty @ 200% in respect of addition of Rs. 642,54,22,000/-

22. Your reply on the merits of the case should reach this office by 22.06.2016, failing which it shall be presumed that you have nothing to state in the matter and the decision in the matter will be taken *ex parte* and on merits.

Yours faithfully,

Encls : As above.

(Bhupinderjit Kumar)
Dy. Commissioner of Income Tax
Circle-18(1), New Delhi

Annex 5: IT reports on NDTV shell companies

INCOME TAX DEPARTMENT

Name of the Assessee	:	**M/s. RRPR Holding Private Limited**
		E-186, Greater Kailash-I,
		New Delhi – 110 048.
Assessment Year	:	2009-10
PAN	:	AADCR1710Q
Status	:	Company
Date	:	29.12.2015

Disposal of Objections In Respect of Reasons Recorded Before The Issue of Notice u/s 148 of the Income tax Act, 1961.

Return declaring loss of Rs. 49,01,73,918/- for Assessment Year (hereinafter referred to "AY") 2009-10 was filed by M/s. RRPR Holding Private Limited (hereinafter referred to as the "assessee") on 29.09.2009. The assessment was completed u/s 143(3) of the Act on 30.12.2011 at Nil income. Later on, notice u/s 148 of the Income Tax Act, 1961 (hereinafter referred to as the Act") was issued to the assessee on 08.08.2014.

2. The reasons recorded before the issue of notice u/s 148 are reproduced as under :-

" Information was received by the Department that during the FY 2008-09 relevant to AY 2009-10, the assessee M/s. RRPR Holding Private Limited had raised interest bearing loan from ICICI Bank Limited amounting to Rs. 375 crores @ 19% p.a. interest and out of this loan amount, immediately after disbursal, it granted interest free loans amounting to Rs. 73.91 crores to its Directors.

2. Perusal of the assessment record of the assessee for AY 2009-10 reveals that return declaring loss of Rs. 49,01,73,918/- for AY 2009-10 was filed by the assessee M/s. RRPR Holding Private Limited on 29.09.2009. The assessment was completed u/s 143(3) of the Act on 30.12.2011 at an income of Rs. NIL. During the year under consideration, on 14.10.2008, the assessee entered into 'Corporate Rupee Loan Facility Agreement' with ICICI Bank Limited for securing loan amounting to Rs. 375 crores on interest @ 19% p.a. From the copy of account titled 'Interest on Loan Payable (ICICI)' available on record, it is observed that during the year, the assessee has suffered total interest amounting to Rs. 34,95,95,456.94 on this loan.

3. Further, it is noticed that out of the interest bearing loan amount, on 16.10.2008, i.e. immediately after disbursal, the assessee has granted interest free loans amounting to Rs. 20,92,00,009.41 and Rs. 71,00,00,107/- to Dr. Prannoy Roy and Mrs. Radhika Roy respectively, who are the assessee's Directors as well as shareholders. It is also noticed that grant of interest free loans out of the interest bearing loan, the assessee suffered interest amounting to Rs. 2,00,81,060/- on account of such loan granted to Dr. Prannoy Roy and interest amounting to Rs. 6,74,50,010/- on account of such loan granted to Mrs. Radhika Roy. This arrangement resulted in a debit balance of Rs. 2,91,86,738/- against Dr. Prannoy Roy and a debit balance of Rs. 70,99,81,710/- against Mrs. Radhika Roy in the account books of the assessee M/s. RRPR Holding

-Disposal of Objections in the case of M/s. RRPR Holding Private Limited for AY 2009-10-

8.1   The relevant extract of section 147 of the Act is reproduced as under :-

"[Income escaping assessment.

147. If the [Assessing] Officer [has reason to believe] that any income chargeable to tax has escaped assessment for any assessment year, he may, subject to the provisions of sections 148 to 153, assess or reassess such income and also any other income chargeable to tax which has escaped assessment and which comes to his notice subsequently in the course of the proceedings under this section, or recompute the loss or the depreciation allowance or any other allowance, as the case may be, for the assessment year concerned (hereafter in this section and in sections 148 to 153 referred to as the relevant assessment year) :

Provided that where an assessment under sub-section (3) of section 143 or this section has been made for the relevant assessment year, no action shall be taken under this section after the expiry of four years from the end of the relevant assessment year, unless any income chargeable to tax has escaped assessment for such assessment year by reason of the failure on the part of the assessee to make a return under section 139

or in response to a notice issued under sub-section (1) of section 142 or section 148 or to disclose fully and truly all material facts necessary for his assessment, for that assessment year:
..."

8.2   Prior to 1989, section 147 provided for two grounds to reopen concluded assessments :-

(i)   On basis of information received by the Assessing Officer, assessment could be reopened. This had to be within four years.

(ii)   Where facts material for assessment are not disclosed in the course of assessment, whether within or beyond four years.

8.3   Supervening these two requirements in the alternative, the initial condition is that the Assessing Officer has reason to believe that there is escapement of income. The first requirement regarding information is now dropped by 1989 amendment and therefore for reopening of assessment within a period of 4 years from the end of assessment year, the only requirement is "reason to believe". For a period of 4 years, further requirement was the non-disclosure of material facts necessary for assessment by the assessee.

8.4   A perusal of the reasons recorded before the issue of notice u/s 148 would reveal that the reopening has been made on account of reason to believe that the taxable income of the assessee amounting to Rs. 6,43,69,252/- has escaped assessment for AY 2009-10. The brief facts of the case are that during the year under consideration, the assessee had entered into 'Corporate Rupee Loan Facility Agreement' with ICICI Bank Limited for securing loan amounting to Rs. 375 crores on interest @ 19% p.a. Immediately after disbursal, on 16.10.2008, the assessee granted interest free loans amounting to Rs. 20,92,00,009.41 and Rs. 71,00,00,107/- to Dr. Prannoy Roy and Mrs. Radhika Roy respectively, who are the assessee's Directors as well as shareholders. On this grant of interest free loans out of the interest bearing loan, the assessee suffered interest amounting to Rs. 2,00,81,060/- on account of such loan granted to Dr. Prannoy Roy and interest amounting to Rs. 6,74,50,010/- on account of such loan granted to Mrs. Radhika Roy. This arrangement resulted in a debit balance of Rs. 2,91,86,738/- against Dr. Prannoy Roy and a debit balance of Rs. 70,99,81,710/- against Mrs. Radhika Roy in the account books of the assessee. No interest was charged by the assessee company on these debit balances although the assessee fully suffered total interest amounting to Rs. 34,95,95,456.94 on this ICICI Bank Loan obtained.

-Disposal of Objections in the case of M/s. RRPR Holding Private Limited for AY 2009-10-

.Ience, the proportionate amount of interest amounting to Rs. 6,43,69,252/-, which the assessee suffered on account of such interest free loans, which was not for business purpose, had to be disallowed being not in accordance with the provisions of u/s 36(1)(iii) of the Act and this amount was to be added to the taxable income of the assessee.

8.5 Now the issue is as to whether on the basis of records it can be said that during the original assessment proceedings u/s 143(3), the assessee had disclosed fully and truly all facts material for assessment on this issue in its case.

8.6 The assessee has stated in its letter containing objections that the following details were filed by it before the AO during the original assessment proceedings :-

S. No.	Document which the assessee claims to have filed	Factual Position in this regard
1	Bank statements of all bank accounts are claimed to have been filed during the assessment proceedings vide letter dated 21.11.2011. The bank statement of syndicate bank a/c no. 6971 and ICICI bank a/c no. 75465 are thus claimed to have been filed. (Copy of letter dated 21.11.2011 is enclosed as Annexure-I)	The claim made by the assessee is factually incorrect. The letter dated 21.11.2011 is on record, but it is different from the copy annexed by the assessee along with its objections, because in the actual letter on record, the assessee had mentioned that it was enclosing copy of bank account of ICICI Bank, which, the AO noticed, was not actually enclosed. Therefore, on the original letter on record, the AR of the assessee has struck off the words "and ICICI Bank" and has also signed on such cutting.

Further, the AO also made an entry in the note sheet on 21.11.2011 that bank statement in respect of account in ICICI Bank, although sought, was yet to be given by the assessee. Again on 25.11.2011, there is an entry in the note sheet that the bank statement of ICICI Bank was not traceable yet. Both these entries are duly signed by the AR of the assessee.

Perusal of the record reveals that even after 25.11.2011, the copy of bank statement of ICICI Bank was not furnished at all.

Thus, it is evident that the assessee's claim of having furnished the impugned details is factually incorrect. |
| 2 | All demat account statements are claimed to have been filed during the assessment proceedings vide letter dated 22.09.2011 (Copy of letter is enclosed as Annexure-II) | At the outset, it is pertinent to mention that copy of bank account of ICICI Bank stated to have been enclosed at sr. no. 1 of letter dated 22.09.2011 was not actually enclosed.

Further, the AO recorded on 22.09.2011 in the note sheet that only part details were furnished and the AR was asked to furnish the details in proper format with page numbering and annexures. It was specifically recorded that complete details were not furnished. Further, it was pointed out that legible copy of the offer document was required and that it was not signed |

NDTV FRAUDS

		by any party and letter of acceptance was also blank. The AR was hence asked to provide the same. Later, on 13.10.2011, the AO recorded in the note sheet that **the AR had stated that declaration had not been signed by the acquirer in the letter of offer and no such signed copy was available with the assessee.** The note sheet is duly signed by the AR also. From the above, it is obvious that the assessee's claim of having furnished the impugned details is factually incorrect.
3	All ledger accounts as part of the complete books of accounts are claimed to have been filed during the assessment proceedings vide letter dated 11.08.2011 and the books of accounts on CD are also claimed to have been submitted vide our letter dated 07.10.2011. (Copy of letters are enclosed as Annexure-III)	**The claim of the assessee is factually incorrect.** Letter dated 11.08.2011 is on record and the ledger accounts regarding interest expenses and other expenses were enclosed. However, letter dated 07.10.2011 is also on record, wherein it is claimed that books of accounts in tally in CD are enclosed, but there is no CD enclosed or on record. Further, **the AO has specifically recorded and the AR of the assessee has confirmed it by placing his signatures in the note sheet on 07.10.2011 that the AR had brought the CD, but the same was not functioning.** Hence, the assessee's claim of having furnished the impugned details is factually incorrect.
4	The details of interest income are claimed to have been filed vide letter dated 27.12.2011 and interest expenses vide letter dated 11.08.2011. (Copies of letters are enclosed as Annexure-IV)	The letters are on record.
5	Detailed explanation was sought by the AO for interest free loans given to directors on 13.09.2011 and the same was replied to in detail vide reply dated 21.10.2011 (Copy of letter is enclosed as Annexure-V)	There is no letter dated 21.10.2011. However, the letter annexed by the assessee as Annexure-V is available on record as letter dated 13.10.2011.

8.7   From the above chart, it can be observed that only part details were furnished by the assessee during the original assessment proceedings and the assessee did not furnish certain information and details at all, which included the following material information :-

    (i)   Copy of bank statement regarding the assessee's bank account with ICICI Bank was not furnished at all.

    (ii)   The assessee never furnished its books of accounts in CD as claimed by it.

8.8   Thus, the contention raised by the assessee that there was no failure on the part of assessee to disclose fully in truly all material facts relevant for assessment, is not correct. As such, the decisions of various Hon'ble Courts cited by the assessee are of no help to it, because the same are on different facts.

-Disposal of Objections in the case of M/s. RRPR Holding Private Limited for AY 2009-10-

8.9   In view of the above, the assessee's claim that it had disclosed fully and truly all material facts necessary for assessment, is not correct.

9. Objection (ii):   Same expenses cannot be disallowed twice.

9.1   The assessee has contended that it had incurred expenses of Rs. 67.52 crore on account of interest on loan and other expenses, out of which the AO appropriated Rs. 1.01 crore towards expenses incurred on earning the interest income of Rs. 1,12,72,344/- and the balance expenses of Rs. 66.51 crore were disallowed u/s 14A of the Act. Hence, the assessee has contended that as there are no expenses, which remained, therefore, there could be no further disallowance as proposed in the reasons.

9.2   On this issue, it is observed that the AO had made the impugned disallowance u/s 14A, which is the subject matter of appeal before the Hon'ble ITAT. The fate of the said addition has not crystallized or become final. Moreover, no addition was made on account of disallowance of expenses, hence, the amount of Rs. 6,43,69,252/-, being the inadmissible interest expenses, has escaped assessment. Accordingly, the income of the assessee which has escaped assessment on account of disallowance out of interest expenses, is required to be assessed now.

9.3   In view of the above, the assessee's contention on this issue is not correct.

10.   As held by various Hon'ble Courts, there has to be prima facie some material on the basis of which the Department could reopen the case. Though the objections have been discussed in detail on the basis of facts also, the sufficiency or final correctness of the material is not a thing to be considered at this stage. And once 'prima facie some material' is present, the Department is not precluded from reopening the assessment. Further, the assessee may present its arguments in detail during the assessment proceedings. And these will be duly considered before completing the assessment.

11.   In view of the above detailed discussion, and after considering the facts of all the cases/judgments cited by the assessee and the submission made by the assessee, the objections raised by the assessee are not found sustainable and the same are hereby rejected and thus stand disposed of. The notice issued u/s 148 of the Income Tax Act, 1961 dated 08.08.2014 is proper and as per law. Therefore, the connected reassessment proceedings u/s 147/148 of the Act, need to be proceeded further. Hence, the reassessment proceedings u/s 147/148 of the Act, are being carried forward as per the provisions of the Income Tax Act, 1961 and Income Tax Rules, 1962.

Sd/-

Dated : 29.12.2015   **(Bhupinderjit Kumar)**
                                                         Dy. Commissioner of Income Tax
                                                         Cir. 18(1), New Delhi

Copy to the assessee :-

Sd/-

Dy. Commissioner of Income Tax
Cir. 18(1), New Delhi

INCOME TAX DEPARTMENT

Name of the Assessee	:	**M/s.RRPR Holding Private Limited** E-186, Greater Kailash-I, New Delhi – 110 048.
Assessment Year	:	2010-11
PAN	:	AADCR1710Q
Status	:	Company
Date	:	29.01.2016

Disposal of Objections In Respect of Reasons Recorded Before The Issue of Notice u/s 148 of the Income tax Act, 1961

Return declaring loss of Rs. 4,17,005/- for Assessment Year (hereinafter referred to as "**AY**") 2010-11 was filed by M/s. RRPR Holding Private Limited (hereinafter referred to as the "**assessee/RRPR**") on 15.10.2010. The assessment was completed u/s 143(3) of the Act on 30.03.2013 at an income of Rs. 30,61,180/-. Later on, notice u/s 148 of the Income Tax Act, 1961 (hereinafter referred to as "**the Act**") was issued to the assessee on 23.03.2015.

2.   The reasons recorded before the issue of notice u/s 148 are reproduced as under :-

"Reasons for reopening of assessment in the case of Ms/ RRPR Holding Private Limited A.Y. 2010-11.

Assessment u/s 143(3) of the Income-tax Act was completed in this case on 30.03.2013 making an addition of Rs.26,44,176/- on account of interest income which was not shown as income from other sources and interest expense was netted off without routing the same in the profit and loss account. The interest income came to the notice to the Assessing Officer from Individual Transaction Data of the assessee company AIR information received.

Subsequent to the assessment proceedings certain information has been received by way of TEPs and also from the details filed by the assessee subsequently in the course of assessment proceeding for later assessment years. The following form the basis for reason to believe that the substantial income has escaped the assessment for the A.Y.2010-11.

1. *M/s RRPL Holding Private Limited is a domestic company incorporated in 19.08.2005 with paid up share capital of Rs.1 lac. Mrs. Radhika Roy and Mr. Pronoy Roy hold 50% equity each in the said company. The assessee company has had no other asset other than shares of listed company-NDTV Limited. In the quarter ending on September, 2008, the company acquired 47,41,721 shares comprising of 7.57% of shareholding of NDTV Limited for a price of Rs.439 per share through open offer in July 2008 and the total stake of PAC i.e. RR, PR and RRPL in NDTV Limited as on 30th September, 2008 was 63.23%.The fund for purchase of these shares came from bank loan initially by India Bulls and later by ICICI Bank vide agreement dated 14.10.2008.*

2. *On 03.08.2009, RRPR Pvt. Limited purchased 115,63,684 shares of Listed Company NDTV Limited from RR and PR at a price of Rs.4 per shares. The market price of the share as per closing price on that date was Rs.139.30/- shares. The stake of RRPR Holding Private Limited became 26% and that of RR and PR reduced to 37.17% in NDTV Limited. As such a valuable right in NDTV comprising of 26% of voting rights was given in RRPR Pvt. Limited. The assessee in effect became an entity in control of NDTV and a critical "SPV/Device/Corporate Vehicle" to control the listed company and also a means of selling/transferring the valuable management right attached with 26% stake of NDTV Limited. The market value of 26% stake in NDTV (16305404 shares) was Rs.228.24/- crores at Rs.140 per share on 05.08.2009. The details of transactions given by the assessee during the year is as under:-*

142

-Disposal of Objections in the case of M/s. RRPR Holding Private Limited for AY 2010-11-

Date	Particulars	Whether through Stock Exchange or off market	No. of Shares	Total Cost of acquisition	Cost per Share	Commutative Balance
01.04.2009	Opening Balance		47,41,721	2,08,15,20,685	438.98	47,41,721
03.08.2009	Shares acquired from Mrs. Radhika Roy	Off Market	57,81,841	2,31,27,364	4.00	1,05,23,562
03.08.2009	Shares acquired from Dr. Prannoy Roy	Off Market	57,81,842	2,31,27.368	4.00	1,63,05.404
08.03.2010	Shares sold to Mrs. Radhika Roy	Off Market	(34,78,925)	(1,39,15,700)	4.00	1,28,26,479
08.03.2010	Shares sold to Dr. Prannoy Roy	Off Market	(34,78,925)	(1,39,15,700)	4.00	93,47.554
08.03.2010	Shares acquired from, Joint A/c	Off Market	48,36,850	67,71,59.000	140	1,41,84,404
08.03.2010	Shares acquired From Mrs.Radhika Roy	Off Market	23,14,762	32,40,66,680	140	1,64,99,166
08.03.2010	Shares acquired from Dr. Prannoy Ray	Off Market	23,14,762	32,40,66.680	140	1.88,13,928
	Total		1,88,13,928	3,42,52,36.377		

3. The above transaction was reported to the stock exchange on 05.08.2009. However, on 21/07/2009, a loan agreement was entered into with Viswapradhan Commercial Private Limited (VCPL), whereby the assessee received Rs.403.85 crores 0% unsecured loan. The amount received from VCPL in two tranches first on 06/08/2009 amounting to Rs.350 crores which was immediately utilized for repayment of bank liability and second on 09.03.2010 utilized in purchase of shares from the promoters. However, it has come to the notice now that the ICICI bank had issued a certificate dated 07/08/2009 that its liability on the assessee is fully repaid. In contradiction to the above certificate, the assessee in all its subsequent balance sheet is still showing long term loan from bank at Rs.44,053,877/-.

4. The terms of the loan agreement filed during the course of the proceedings for A.Y.2010-13 clearly show that VCPL by giving an amount of Rs.403.85 crores acquired the option to convert the loan into such number of equity shares at par aggregating to 99.99% of the fully diluted share capital of RRPR Holding at any time. The terms of loan stated that the money received shall compulsorily be utilized for retiring the bank liability appearing in the books of the company. Clause 3 of the agreement defined 'Authorized Purpose' as under:-

"The Borrower shall utilize the loan in full for repayment of an existing loan availed by the borrowers from ICICI bank Limited pursuant to a loan agreement executed between ICICI Bank and the Borrower dated 14th October, 2008."

5. Clause 6.1 of the agreement states that

" The borrower shall issue a convertible warrant (the Warrant), convertible into equity shares aggregating to 99.99% of the fully diluted Equity Share Capital of the borrower at the time of the conversion to the Lender immediately upon execution of the agreement. The warrant shall be subject to terms and conditions set out in schedule 1." Clause 6.2 states that
" The lender shall have the right to purchase from the promoters all the equity shares of the borrower held by promoter at par value."

As stated above the share capital of the assessee company is only Rs.1 lac. Hence for Rs.1 lac at par value the assessee company is de facto getting transferred alongwith 26% stake in NDTV Limited as on the date of the agreement. Thus from the terms of the agreement, it is clear that controlling stake (valuable stake) in NDTV Limited has been transferred to the lender and merely formality of conversion is to take place on papers. The purpose of the receipt of the money is used is predetermined.

143

-Disposal of Objections in the case of M/s. RRPR Holding Private Limited for AY 2010-11-

6. Schedule 1 under the head 'Terms of the Warrant' at clause (a) states that " At the sole option of the lender, the warrant may be converted , into such number of equity shares at par aggregating to 99.99% of the fully diluted equity share capital at the time of conversion of the borrower at any time during the tenure of the Loan or thereafter without requiring any further act or deed on the part of the assessee. From the above terms it is clear that irrespective of the repayment of loan or otherwise, the right over the assessee has been transferred to the assessee. Repayment of loan would not absolve the right of the lender to have control over the assets of the assessee. The Lender thus has obtained an irrevocable right /warrant to acquire RRPR (99.99%) at a mere consideration of Rs.1lac and this transaction was put into effect immediately on 27.07.2009. Irrespective of repayment of loan the ownership change of NDTV shares via the transfer of RRPR will remain and is not dependent upon any event and cannot be reversed. This shows that the entire arrangement was designed to effect transfer of 26% of stake in NDTV through RRPR for a pittance consideration of Rs.1 lac.

7. The terms of loan agreement thus indicate that the loan received is nothing but consideration for transfer of 26% of the shares of NDTV Limited and also the valuable rights by virtue of such huge stake. This is very clear from clause 2(a) of schedule 3 of the Agreement, which specifes that the promoters of NDTV or NDTV group shall require prior written consent of the Lender to " issue any equity securities of NDTV which results in the aggregate valuation of NDTV being less than Rs.1346 crores.(valuation at which the Lender has put into money into the Company). The amount in the loan agreement is shown at Rs.350 crores . This comes to exactly 26% of the valuation of the NDTV arrived by the assessee for the purpose of acquiring. This also coincides with the pre-condition in clause 9.2(e) of the agreement that RRPR must hold 26% stake in NDTV Limited.

8. It is noticed that RR and PR transferred their stake (18.44% in NDTV) merely for Rs.4 per shares so that the company could have 26% of the stake. The right over 26% stakes in NDTV was thus transferred to the lender by way of the terms of agreement. The stake of the company in NDTV Limited has been further increased to 29.18% on 09.03.2010 with addition of 3.18% shares at a price of Rs.4 per share purchased by the assessee from Radhika Roy and Pronoy Roy.

9. The fact that the promoters transferred their stake 18.44% merely for Rs.4 was put to question during the course of the assessment proceedings for A.Y.2010-11. In reply thereto, the assessee vide letter dated 06/03/2013 stated that the promoters shares were transferred to the assessee because the value of shares held as pledge by ICICI Bank has declined considerably and their shares have to be transferred to save the investment.

The assessee had stated " ...As the assessee had to repay the loan of Indo Bulls Securities Limited , which it had borrowed for acquiring the shares of NDTV Ltd and as the prices have crashed the value of shares held by the assessee were not sufficient to offer as security to new lender viz. ICICI Bank. As the directors of the assessee company were the only shareholders of the assessee company, they brought in their personal shares 1,15,63,683 shares of NDTV Ltd in the assessee company at a face value of Rs.4/- per share..."

10. This was a misstatement as the assessee must be well aware of the fact that it has negotiated to receive 0% unsecured loan of Rs.403.85 crores from VCPL. The loan agreement was signed almost simultaneously on 05/08/2009.Thus the claim that the shares were purchased to save the investment of the company is not correct.

11. From the above, it is clear that the promoter of RRPR Holding Pvt. Limited, i.e. Mrs. RR and Mr. PR transferred through colorable sham transaction, the right over NDTV Limited held through RRPR Holding Private Limited. Prior to this transfer on 05.08.2009, Mrs.Radhika Roy and Pronnoy Ray were holding 55.6% of total holding of NDTV (23.75% by PR, 24.14% by RR and 7.71% in their joint account).

Thus, RR and PR no longer have controlling stake in NDTV Limited and apparently no consideration was shown to have received directly in lieu of transfer of their controlling rights in NDTV Limited, by way of transfer of the assessee company.

12. As stated above, in the reply filed during the course of assessment proceedings on 06/03/2013 the assessee company stated that this transaction was for making good the value of security held by the bank because the same has dipped as the market value of NDTV stock declined considerably during the time. At the same time, from the facts available on record, it is crystal clear that the shares at a price of Rs.4 per share were transferred to the assessee company, much below the market price solely for the reason that the stake of the company should reach 26%. Only then, VCPL agreed to infuse funds as loan convertible into share capital. If these shares were not transferred at

-Disposal of Objections in the case of M/s. RRPR Holding Private Limited for AY 2010-11-

such a low price, either the assessee company would have lost its assets to bank as stated by the assessee, or the company would have had to purchased these shores from market at market value in order to have the funds infused from VCPL. The VCPL funding was with the condition that company should hold 26% stake. The assessee apparently had no fund but had to purchase the same. The purchase of the shares at credit, at market price even from promoters would have created a liability in the hands of the company by way of difference of market price and actual price paid. The assessee avoided the situation by entering into a self serving transaction with promoters which saved its business. The amount of liability avoided by it or the amount of liability waived by the promoters, by way of entering into such transaction definitely provided benefit of equal amount to the assessee in the course of its business. This cannot be seen as a notional benefit but indeed is a real benefit. The benefit is towards working capital of the company for saving of its only current assets namely shares of NDTV. The company also saved in addition to working capital, interest on loan amount which would have been chargeable had the company acquired such benefit by raising liability for working capital with market rate of interest. The assessee company itself has been claiming that it is into the business of making investment with having sole asset of share of NDTV and also claiming interest expenses. The disallowance of interest expense as the income is to be exempted or taxable under special method for computation of income under the head capital gains does not preclude the fact that the assessee is in the business of investment of holding its subsidiary. The Memorandum of association of the company also states the same fact.

In view of the above, it is seen that the assessee company received a direct and tangible benefit arising from the course of its business. The benefit is real one capable of characterized as 'income' and not a notional benefit.

13. It is further noticed that as on August 5,2009, the value of asset/NAV in the books of the assessee was 26% shares of NDTV Ltd only, which would be around Rs.210 crores. The assessee company however received a consideration of Rs.403.85 crores in the form of 0% convertible unsecured loan and the entire proceeds were used to extinguish a liability of loan and interest to ICICI bank. Thus RRPR immediately benefited by Rs.400 crore i.e 400 crores less Rs.4.62 crores being cost of asset acquired on the same date. This sale consideration has been camouflaged as issue of convertible debenture for avoiding payment of tax on actual transfer of 26% holding in NDTV Limited.

Source of loan fund received and anomalies noticed

14. The alleged loan received from VCPL amounting to Rs.403.85 crores was found to be belonging to Reliance Group (Mukesh Ambani). However, subsequently in a public statement, Reliance Group has denied having any interest in RRPR Holding Private Limited. This is referred to in an article published by www.newslaundry.com.Denial of having given any loan by the lender casts shadow over the nature of the transaction and makes the said liable to be taxed as unexplained cash credit. During the course of assessment proceedings for A.Y.12-13, the assessee company was categorically asked to furnish:-
   i. Complete copy of loan agreement along with all annexures including changes in terms or modification if any.
   ii. Who are the promoters of the person giving you unsecured loan. Details of key persons and share holders of the concern may please be given.
   iii. How the interest free loan was secured from an unrelated party. The same may kindly be explained in the light of the fact that prior to availing this loan; you had to pay huge interest to fund the investments in your subsidiary. Please also give the details of person who helped you procure the loan.
   iv. Copies of documents/notes exchanged in finalizing the terms of the loan may also be furnished.
   v. Please state whether you or your directors or any related concern has had any transaction with the person giving you the unsecured loan or any of their directors, share holders or related/associate concerns. If yes, please give the details and if no please furnish a categorical denial.
   vi. Is the person giving loan is related to any other Industrial House. If yes please give the details.
   vii. Please give the current status as on date of the unsecured loan shown as outstanding as on 31.03.2012.

15. In reply to the above pointed questions, the assessee merely submitted letter dated 10.02.2015 in which it has given the details of director and shareholder of VCPL and stated that loan agreement is only available document in this regard. Interestingly, the assessee company categorically stated that it is not aware whether the lending company is related to any industrial house. The above facts clearly show that the assessee is not forthcoming with its replies. The person extending such a huge interest free loan is whether related to any industrial house is, as per the assessee, not known to it. This is despite the fact that the person signing the agreement Sh. K.R. Raja is one of key personnel of Reliance Group at the time of signing of agreement.

NDTV FRAUDS

.6. *As per the report of the DGIT(Investigation) dated 10.05.2011 available on record, it is seen the share capital of VCPL was Rs.1 lac only and it has raised the fund by way of "zero coupon optionally convertible loan" of Rs.403.85 crores from its related company Shinano Retail Private Limited which is a Reliance Group (Mukesh Ambani). The DGIT investigation has gone into the source of funds of Shinano Retail, which were Reliance Port and Terminal Limited and Reliance Ventures Limited etc, which were found assessed at Mumbai respectively in the report.*

As per the new information received, the zero coupon optionally convertible loan given to VCPL was converted into Zero Coupon Optionally Convertible Debenture (OCD) on 30.06.2012 by Shinano Retail. In March 2012, i.e F.Y.11-12, the debenture of Rs.403.85 crores was sold by Shinano to M/s Eminent Network Private Limited for Rs.50 crores. Why Shinano Retail booked the loss on sale of debenture and whether claimed the same as deduction is not known M/s Eminent Network Private Limited is owned by M/s Digivision Cable which is in turn a subsidiary of HFCL as per last information available. Thus it is seen that loan worth Rs.403.85 crores has been acquired by an entity merely for Rs.50 crores. The facts narrated above indicate that the transaction is not a straight forward business transaction, but a convoluted one. The nature and source of transaction is thus not explainable and therefore comes within the ambit of the provisions of section 68 of the Income Tax Act.

17. *Transaction with ICICI bank and disclosures in Balance Sheet*

The assessee company had received a loan of Rs.375 crores vide facility agreement dated 14.10.2008. This money was utilized to acquire shares of NDTV Limited. The liability of the bank was fully extinguished by the assessee on receipt of the unsecured loan from VCPL on 05.08.2009. The ICICI Bank vide letter dated August 7, 2009 confirmed to RRPR Holding that the entire amount due and payable by the company in respect of agreement dated 14.10.2008 has been repaid in full. It is surprising to note that on 06.08.2009, the ICICI Bank had issued an Amendatory Credit Arrangement Letter revising the interest rate of term loan of Rs.375 crore at 9.659% per annum from the date of the first disbursement. The first disbursement was made in F.Y. 2008-09. In addition to the above a fee of Rs.10 crores payable on market capitalization of NDTV touching Rs.20.00 billion and a further fee of Rs.5 crore payable upon market capitalization touching Rs.25.00 billion in cash or NDTV shares of equivalent value was stipulated.

This is in blatant contradiction with the letter dated 07.08.2009 a day after this amendatory credit arrangement letter was entered into. This further contradicts letter of 7/8/2009, which said the loan is fully paid. At the same time note no.10 of balance sheet of 2014, Rs.4.45 crores is still being shown outstanding towards ICICI Bank.

18. *Interest Payment to ICICI Bank*

Assessment proceedings for A.Y.209-10 has been reopened on the ground that the assessee company had claimed interest payment of Rs.39.06 crores on loan of Rs.375 crores taken from ICICI Bank at the rate of 19.5%. Part of the interest bearing fund was forwarded to the directors Ms. Radhika Roy and Mr. Pronnoy Roy without charging of interest. It is seen that new interest free 0% unsecured loan was received from VSPL on 07/08/2009. Thus the assessee was liable to make payment of interest to ICICI Bank till the loan amount is repaid, which happened on 07/08/2009. However, in the balance sheet filed, there is not accounting entry relating to interest liability for the period 01.04.2009 to 07.08.2009. As such, it is noticed that the balance sheet of the assessee is not reflecting the correct state of the financial affairs of the assessee company.

In view of the above, it is clear that income chargeable to tax has escaped assessment within the meaning of section 147 of the Income Tax Act. Since the case falls under the provision of section 151(1) of the Act, notice under section 148 of the Act is hereby issued."

3. The jurisdiction over the case was transferred from Circle-20(2), New Delhi to Circle-18(1), New Delhi vide order F.No. PCIT-07/Centralization/F-38/2015-16/487 dated 29.07.2015 passed u/s 127 of the Act by the Principal Commissioner of Income Tax-07, New Delhi. Thereafter, vide letter no. 307 dated 20.08.2015, it was pointed out to the assessee that no return in response to notice u/s 148 had been filed by it and the assessee was requested to file return in response to notice u/s 148. As no reply was received, therefore, vide letter no. 536 dated 03.09.2015, the assessee was asked to show cause as to why proceedings u/s 276CC may not be initiated for non-compliance of notice u/s 148.

-Disposal of Objections in the case of M/s. RRPR Holding Private Limited for AY 2010-11-

4.   In response, the assessee filed reply on 10.09.2015 stating that it had stated vide an earlier letter dated 08.04.2015 that revised return filed on 02.02.2012 for AY 2010-11 may be treated as return in response to notice u/s 148. Further, the assessee also filed return electronically on 09.09.2015 in response to notice u/s 148 of the Act. As the assessee also requested for supply of reasons recorded before issue of notice u/s 148, therefore, copy of such reasons was supplied to the assessee vide letter dated 06.10.2015. Thereafter, vide letter filed on 04.11.2015, the assessee filed objections to the assumption of jurisdiction u/s 147 of the Act in its case for AY 2010-11.

5.   Before taking up the various objections raised by the assessee, it is appropriate to discuss the facts of the case, which are detailed hereunder.

5.1   The assessee company RRPR was incorporated on 19.08.2005 with a capital of Rs. 1 lac. Dr. Prannoy Roy and Mrs. Radhika Roy are the directors and shareholders in RRPR, having 50% share each. RRPR is the holding company of M/s. New Delhi Television Limited ("NDTV") and has no other assets except the shares of NDTV. The shares of NDTV were acquired by RRPR as follows :-

Date	Particulars	No. of shares	Cost per share (in Rs.)	Total cost of acquisition	Cumulative Balance	%age of stake in NDTV
03.07.2008	Purchased in open offer	97,95,434	438.98	429,99,99,618	97,95,434	15.64
14.07.2008	Sold	(38,03,728)	446	1,69,73,38,496	59,91,706	9.55
08.08.2008	Sold	(12,49,985)	409	51,07,03,247	47,41,721	7.56
03.08.2009	Purchased from Mrs. Radhika Roy	57,81,841	4	2,31,27,364	1,05,23,562	16.78
03.08.2009	Purchased from Dr. Prannoy Roy	57,81,842	4	2,31,27.368	1,63,05,404	26%
08.03.2010	Shares sold to Mrs. Radhika Roy	(34,78,925)	4	1,39,15,700	1,28,26,479	20.45
08.03.2010	Shares sold to Dr. Prannoy Roy	(34,78,925)	4	1,39,15,700	93,47,554	14.50
08.03.2010	Purchased from Joint A/c	48,36,850	140	67,71,59.000	1,41,84,404	22
08.03.2010	Purchased from Mrs.Radhika Roy	23,14,762	140	32,40,66,680	1,64,99,166	25.60
08.03.2010	Purchased from Dr. Prannoy Roy	23,14,762	140	32,40,66.680	1,88,13,928	29.19

5.2   From the above, it is evident that prior to 03.08.2009, RRPR was having only 7.56% stake in NDTV. On 21.07.2009, RRPR entered into an agreement with Vishwapradhan Commercial Private Limited ("VCPL"), which was titled as "Loan Agreement dated 21.07.2009 between VCPL and RRPR and Prannoy Roy and Radhika Roy". **This agreement was not furnished by the assessee during the assessment proceedings for AY 2010-11, which were completed on 30.03.2013.**

5.3   Subsequent to the completion of assessment for AY 2010-11 on 30.03.2013, fresh information surfaced from the following three sources :-

Source 1   Tax Evasion Petitions ("TEPs") received from a shareholder of NDTV from 29.06.2013 onwards.

147

NDTV FRAUDS

Source 2   Copy of loan agreement regarding receipt of interest free loan of Rs. 403.85 crore by the assessee titled as "Loan Agreement dated 21.07.2009 between VCPL and RRPR and Prannoy Roy and Radhika Roy" was furnished by the assessee company for the first time along with its reply dated 10.02.2015 filed during the course of assessment proceedings for AY 2012-13.

Source 3   The article dated 14.01.2015 published on the website www.newslaundry.com, which corroborated the facts and the dubious nature of transaction of receipt of interest free loan of Rs. 403.85 crore by the assessee.

5.4   It is revealed from careful perusal of the terms and conditions of alleged loan agreement for the first time during assessment proceedings for subsequent AY 2012-13 that RRPR had transferred its controlling interest in NDTV for Rs. 403.85 crore to VCPL through following three step processes :

> **Step 1** RRPR having paid up capital of Rs. 1 lac acquired controlling interest in NDTV for Rs. 403.85 crore taking huge loan.
>
> **Step 2** Controlling interest of RRPR in NDTV was transferred to VCPL for Rs. 403.85 crore.
>
> **Step 3** Loan taken by RRPR to buy controlling interest in NDTV was repaid. However, in order to avoid gain from transfer of controlling interest to VCPL, payment was camouflaged as loan agreement, which was essentially a sale agreement in substance as evident from peculiar terms and conditions of the agreement. It is incomprehensible that VCPL will give loan of Rs. 403.85 crore to RRPR without charging any interest. No prudent businessman will engage in such transaction unless and until it is for acquisition, which is evident from other terms and conditions of the agreement.

5.5   The above said agreement although purported to be a loan agreement contained the following clauses :-

(i)   The consideration passed is interest free. Nobody would lend Rs. 403.85 crore without charging any interest unless the amount is actually consideration for acquisition of asset and not a loan.

(ii)   The above is further corroborated from the stipulation in the agreement that VCPL acquired the option to convert the loan into such number of equity shares at par aggregating to 99.99% of the fully diluted share capital of RRPR at any time.

(iii)   VCPL shall have the right to purchase from the promoters all the equity shares of RRPR held by the promoters at par value, i.e. the entire RRPR will be liable for purchase by VCPL for Rs. 1 lac.

(iv)   The option available with VCPL regarding conversion of loan into 99.99% of the fully diluted share capital of RRPR at any time also extends to the period after repayment of such loan. Repayment of loan does not absolve the assessee from this perpetual option granted to RRPR.

(v)   The agreement stipulates that RRPR shall hold and shall continue to hold 26% shares of NDTV.

(vi)   For the purpose of the impugned agreement, valuation of NDTV has duly been carried out and figure of Rs. 1346 crore has been assigned as value of NDTV.

148

(vii) The amount of Rs. 350 crore recorded in the loan agreement is exactly 26% of the valuation of NDTV.

(viii) The loan is contingent upon completion of due diligence of investment of US $ 85 million by NDTV Four Holdings Limited, Mauritius in NDTV Studios Private Limited and further upon the ability of RRPR to transfer to NTDV and utilize US $ 85 million either by merger of NDTV Studios Private Limited with NDTV or by any other method.

5.6 **From the above referred to peculiar terms and conditions of alleged loan agreement, it was revealed for the first time that the assessee had in fact transferred the controlling interest of NDTV in the hands of RRPR as a first step and had then sold this controlling interest for Rs. 403.85 crore to VCPL by clothing the agreement for sale as a loan agreement.**

5.7 Since the reasons recorded by the AO contain various pieces of information, the same are summarized for the sake of convenience as under :-

Source of information	Stage involved in transaction	Description
Tax evasion complaint & alleged Loan Agreement	Stage 1	Agreement titles "Loan Agreement dated 21.07.2009 between VCPL and RRPR and Prannoy Roy and Radhika Roy" entered into by RRPR & its 2 shareholders with VCPL. One of the conditions in this agreement was that RRPR shall hold and shall continue to hold 26% stake in NDTV.
Tax evasion complaint	Stage 2	(i) On 03.08.2009, RRPR, which was hitherto having a stake of 7.56% only in NDTV, purchased 57,81,841 shares from Mrs. Radhika Roy @ Rs. 4 per share **(when the price listed at BSE was about Rs. 140 per share)**, taking the stake of RRPR in NDTV to 16.78%. (ii) On the same day, RRPR, which now had a stake of 16.78% in NDTV, purchased 57,81,842 shares from Dr. Prannoy Roy @ Rs. 4 per share **(when the price listed at BSE was about Rs. 140 per share)**, taking the stake of RRPR in NDTV to exactly 26%.
Tax evasion complaint & Article in newslaundry website	Stage 3	(i) On 05.08.2009, RRPR paid off entire liability of ICICI Bank by utilizing the amount received from VCPL under the above stated agreement and no due certificate issued by ICICI Bank to RRPR on 07.08.2009. (ii) VCPL got the right over unencumbered assets of RRPR being 26% controlling stake in NDTV by way of optionally convertible 99.99% equity of RRPR at par (i.e. for Rs. 1 lac only). This means that at any time, VCPL could claim 26% controlling ownership of NDTV by paying only Rs. 1 lac.

5.8 On receipt of new and credible information as described above, the AO initiated reassessment proceedings by way of issue of notice u/s 148 of the Act on 23.03.2015.

NDTV FRAUDS

6. In the light of the above facts of the case, the various objections raised by the assessee have been carefully considered and these are discussed in the following paras of the present order.

7. **Comments on general observations made by the assessee before raising specific objections**

7.1 Before raising specific objections, in para 3 of the letter containing objections, the assessee has stated that the reasons recorded are not based on any tangible material so as to form an opinion that income of the assessee has escaped assessment. However, in the same para 3 of the said letter, the assessee has acknowledged that the reasons to believe have been formed on the basis of information received by the AO by way of Tax Evasion Petitions ("TEPs"). It is reiterated that reason to believe of the AO that income has escaped assessment was based on the basis and information received from three sources as discussed in preceding paragraphs. The AO has further analysed this information carefully and has reached a reasonable and logical conclusion that income has escaped assessment as discussed in paragraph 12 and 13 of the reasons.

7.2 Further in para 3, the assessee has raised the contention that it is not the case of the AO that the assessee has failed to make full and true disclosure during the original assessment proceedings. On this issue, it is observed that prior to 1989, section 147 provided for two grounds to reopen concluded assessments :-

(i) On basis of information received by the Assessing Officer, assessment could be reopened. This had to be within four years.

(ii) Where facts material for assessment are not disclosed in the course of assessment, whether within or beyond four years.

7.3 Supervening these two requirements in the alternative, the initial condition is that the Assessing Officer has reason to believe that there is escapement of income. The first requirement regarding information is now dropped by 1989 amendment and therefore for reopening of assessment within a period of 4 years from the end of assessment year, the only requirement is "reason to believe". For a period of 4 years, further requirement was the non-disclosure of material facts necessary for assessment by the assessee.

7.4 **The condition regarding full and true disclosure, which is contained in the 1st Proviso to section 147, applies only to case in which the assessment is sought to be reopened after 4 years from the end of the relevant assessment year. In the assessee's case, the reopening is made within 4 years and hence, the 1st Proviso to section 147 is not applicable in this case.**

7.5 The assessee has also alleged that the AO has not examined all transactions of the assessee as disclosed in its financial statements and hence, the material received by way of TEPs or filed by the assessee in subsequent proceedings could not constitute fresh material for initiation of reassessment proceedings. However, this allegation is bereft of any explanation or supporting argument to substantiate this allegation and hence, the same is without any merit.

7.6 In para 3.1 of the impugned letter, the assessee has again raised allegations that the AO has not specified any material for initiation of reassessment proceedings, without substantiating the allegation and even when the detailed reasons containing 18 paragraphs and running into 7 pages have been duly intimated to the assessee. In para 3.2 to 3.4 of the impugned letter, the assessee has stated that the information on the shape of TEPs, report of DGIT (Investigation) and the article published on the website www.newslaundry.com have not been supplied to the assessee. It is observed that in the earlier letters, the assessee had requested for supply of reasons, which were duly supplied to it and now that the assessee has raised this issue, the relevant extract

150

Sree Iyer

-Disposal of Objections in the case of M/s. RRPR Holding Private Limited for AY 2010-11-

of TEPs and the article published on the website www.newslaundry.com are separately supplied to the assessee vide letter of even date. It is further observed that if any further objections are raised by the assessee pertaining to these documents, the same shall be duly dealt with.

8.   Further, in para 4 onwards in the impugned letter, the assessee has raised five objections to contend that the proceedings initiated u/s 147 are without jurisdiction. These objections are as under :-

S. No.	Gist of Objection	Discussed at para no.
1	That reasons recorded are based on no material much less tangible and relevant material to initiate action u/s 147 of the Act	10
2	That reasons recorded are in any case not based on any fresh tangible material which surfaced after furnishing of return of income and as such, initiation of proceedings u/s 147 of the Act is without jurisdiction.	11
3	That no income has escaped assessment and therefore mandatory precondition for invoking of provision u/s 147 is not satisfied	12
4	That proceedings u/s 147 of the Act are proceedings for investigation and, therefore the action is impermissible	13
5	That proceedings initiated u/s 147 of the Act are based on change of opinion and therefore, instant proceedings are in excess of jurisdiction	14

9.   While considering the above grounds of objections, due consideration has been given to the factual matrix of the case and the legal and judicial position as it exists in view of the various judgments of Hon'ble Apex Court. Each of the above objections is being dealt with, point-wise in the following paras.

10.   **That reasons recorded are based on no material much less tangible and relevant material to initiate action u/s 147 of the Act**

10.1   In para 5.1 of its objections, the assessee has contended that in its case, there is no material much less tangible material, which could enable the AO to form a prima facie belief that the income of the assessee company had escaped assessment. It is interesting to observe that in para 5.2 at page 16 of the objections, the assessee has admitted that the transfer of shares from Dr. Prannoy Roy and Mrs. Radhika Roy were made, because this was a precondition, on which basis VCPL had agreed to grant loan to RRPR. Incidentally, this is exactly what has been recorded in the reasons. Thus, it becomes an undisputed fact that the actual substance of transaction of grant of loan by VCPL to RRPR was the acquisition of 26% controlling stake in NDTV and to achieve this purpose, the deficiency of shares of NDTV in RRPR was made good by transferring the requisite number of shares from Dr. Prannoy Roy and Mrs. Radhika Roy to RRPR.

10.2   Thus, in para 5.1 of its objections, the assessee has made a bald assertion that in the present case, there is no material, which could form the basis of belief regarding income having escaped assessment. However, this assertion is not supported by any facts or other evidence. Contrary to this assertion, it is observed that the AO has specifically recorded in the reasons as under :-

"Subsequent to the assessment proceedings certain information has been received by way of TEPs and also from the details filed by the assessee subsequently in the course of assessment proceeding for later assessment years."

10.2.1 Further, the material forming the basis of belief regarding escapement of income is elaborately discussed in para 5 above, from which it is evident that the most crucial information, which put all pieces of jigsaw puzzle of different transactions in place came from the tax evasion complaints and the loan agreement, both of which were not available to the AO at the time of

Page 10 of 18

NDTV FRAUDS

original assessment. The agreement was most crucial document was the agreement titled as "Loan Agreement dated 21.07.2009 between VCPL and RRPR and Prannoy Roy and Radhika Roy", which was admittedly not filed during the original assessment proceedings. This is without prejudice to the fact that this is a case of reopening within 4 years from end of assessment year, hence, the issue regarding disclosure is not relevant.

10.3   From the above, it is clear that the material forming basis of belief is referred to in the reasons itself and hence, the assessee's contention regarding non-existence of any material is not acceptable. Therefore, the decisions of the Hon'ble Supreme Court referred to by the assessee are also not applicable to the facts of the present case, which are different from the facts of the cited cases.

10.4   In para 5.3 (and repeated again in para 5.21 & 5.22) of the objections, the assessee has referred to the observation of the AO that the long term loan from bank is reflected at Rs. 4,40,50,877/-, whereas it came to notice later that ICICI Bank had issued certificate on 07.08.2009 stating that full liability had been paid by the assessee. The assessee has contended that certain averments in this regard were given in note no. 10 of the audited financial statements. However, it is observed that this objection concerning the interpretation of observations given in the note no. 10 is extraneous to the present proceedings, wherein the matter is not concerning the merits of the case, but regarding the validity of assumption of jurisdiction u/s 147 of the Act. When the main reason for reopening is the transaction of sale of controlling interest in NDTV by RRPR to VCPL, contending about any difference in interpretation on the merits of issue regarding quantum of liability towards ICICI Bank is a digression from the main issue.

10.5   In para 5.4, the assessee has referred to loan agreement with ICICI Bank stated to have been filed during the assessment proceedings and has filed copy of ledger account of ICICI Bank. The assessee has contended that all these documents were duly examined during the assessment proceedings. Again, it is observed that the main reason for reopening is the transaction of sale of controlling interest in NDTV by RRPR to VCPL and filing of agreement with ICICI Bank dated 14.10.2008 is not relevant. It is reiterated that the most crucial document was the agreement titled as "Loan Agreement dated 21.07.2009 between VCPL and RRPR and Prannoy Roy and Radhika Roy", which was admittedly not filed during the original assessment proceedings. This is without prejudice to the fact that this is a case of reopening within 4 years from end of assessment year, hence, the issue regarding disclosure is not relevant.

10.6   Further in para 5.4, the assessee has stated that it had filed copy of certificate dated 17.08.2009 before the ADIT, Unit-II, Inv. Wing on 17.01.2011 before whom complete books of accounts for FYs 2008-09 and 2009-10 were also filed on 30.05.2011. On this issue, it is observed that disclosure of information before an authority other than the Assessing Officer is no defence to reopening of assessment by the AO.

10.7   In view of the above, the assessee's contention that the reopening is without any material and is based on surmises, conjectures and suspicion is incorrect and not acceptable. Further, the assessee has contended in para 5.5 that the agreement with VCPL is a loan agreement and cannot be read as a share transfer agreement.

10.8   On the above issue, it is observed that as already stated in the reasons, although the agreement entered into by RRPR with VCPL is clothed as a loan agreement, yet actually it is an agreement not for grant of loan but for transfer of controlling interest in NDTV through transfer of RRPR itself. This position is evident from the following terms and conditions stipulated in the impugned agreement :-

  (i)   The consideration passed is interest free. Nobody would lend Rs. 403.85 crore without charging any interest unless the amount is actually consideration for acquisition of asset and not a loan.

-Disposal of Objections in the case of M/s. RRPR Holding Private Limited for AY 2010-11-

(ii) The above is further corroborated from the stipulation in the agreement that VCPL acquired the option to convert the loan into such number of equity shares at par aggregating to 99.99% of the fully diluted share capital of RRPR at any time.

(iii) VCPL shall have the right to purchase from the promoters all the equity shares of RRPR held by the promoters at par value, i.e. the entire RRPR will be liable for purchase by VCPL for Rs. 1 lac.

(iv) The option available with VCPL regarding conversion of loan into 99.99% of the fully diluted share capital of RRPR at any time also extends to the period after repayment of such loan. Repayment of loan does not absolve the assessee from this perpetual option granted to RRPR.

(v) The agreement stipulates that RRPR shall hold and shall continue to hold 26% shares of NDTV.

(vi) For the purpose of the impugned agreement, valuation of NDTV has duly been carried out and figure of Rs. 1346 crore has been assigned as value of NDTV.

(vii) The amount of Rs. 350 crore recorded in the loan agreement is exactly 26% of the valuation of NDTV.

(viii) The loan is contingent upon completion of due diligence of investment of US $ 85 million by NDTV Four Holdings Limited, Mauritius in NDTV Studios Private Limited and further upon the ability of RRPR to transfer to NTDV and utilize US $ 85 million either by merger of NDTV Studios Private Limited with NDTV or by any other method.

10.9 It is further contended that confirmation of loan was filed during the assessment proceedings and note on loan was also furnished. This argument is unacceptable, because it is undisputed fact that the alleged loan agreement was not furnished during the assessment proceedings.

10.10 Further, in paras 5.7 to 5.10, the assessee has raised repetitive contentions regarding lack of material, which have already been dealt with in the foregoing paras of this order. The assessee has discussed the contents of replies filed before the AO in the original assessment proceedings to the extent that the provisions of section 28(iv) are not applicable and no benefit accrued to the assessee company or to its Directors as a result of transactions of purchase and sale of shares between themselves. These issues are not relevant in the present matter. The assessee has next referred to similar replies filed before the Investigation Wing, which are again beside the issue involved in the present matter.

10.11 In para 5.11, the assessee has stated that the relationship between the assessee and VCPL is that of debtor and creditor. The assessee has cited the decision of the Hon'ble Supreme Court in the case of ED Sasson & Co. Ltd. Vs CIT 26 ITR 27 SC in this regard. It is observed that in the present case, the issue is that of 'form' and 'substance' and undisputably, the 'substance' shall prevail over 'form'. The substance of the impugned agreement is the acquisition of 26% controlling stake in NDTV through gaining 99.99% equity of RRPR, as discussed in the earlier paras of the present order. Under these circumstances, when apparent is not real, the decision of the Hon'ble Supreme Court shall not help the assessee.

10.12 In para 5.12, the assessee has contended that the statement in the reasons that VCPL had sold the debentures to Eminent Networks P. Ltd. for Rs. 50 crore was not relevant in the assessee's case. In para 5.13, it is again contended that the assessee has borrowed money and what happens afterwards is wholly irrelevant. On this issue, it is observed that when the apparent is not real, the transaction has to be appreciated from all angles. In the case of Workmen,

NDTV FRAUDS

-Disposal of Objections in the case of M/s. RRPR Holding Private Limited for AY 2010-11-

Associated Rubber Industry Limited vs Associated Rubber Industry Limited And Another 157 ITR 77 (SC), the Hon'ble Supreme Court has observed as under :-

> "It is true that in law the Associated Rubber Industry Ltd. and Aril Holdings Ltd. were distinct legal entities having separate existence. But, in our view, that was not an end of the matter. It is the duty of the court, in every case where ingenuity is expended to avoid taxing and welfare legislations, to get behind the smoke-screen and discover the true state of affairs. The court is not to be satisfied with form and leave well alone the substance of a transaction."

10.13 Further, in the above cited case, the Hon'ble Supreme Court observed as follows :-

> "More recently, we have pointed out in McDowell & Co. Ltd. v. Commercial Tax Officer [1985] 3 SCC 230 ; [1985] 154 ITR 148 (SC) at p. 161
>
> " It is up to the court to take stock to determine the nature of the new and sophisticated legal devices to avoid tax and consider whether the situation created by the devices could be related to the existing legislation with the aid of 'emerging' techniques of interpretation as was done in Ramsay's case [1981] 2 WLR 449 ; [1982] AC 300, Burmah Oil [1982] Simon's Tax Cases 30 and Dawson's case [1984] 1 All ER 530; 2 WLR 226 (HL), to expose the devices for what they really are and to refuse to give judicial benediction.""

10.14 In the case of CIT v. Durga Prasad More [1971] 82 ITR 540 (SC), the Hon'ble Supreme Court observed that the taxing authorities are not required to put on blinkers while looking at the documents produced before them. They are entitled to look into the surrounding circumstances to find out the reality of the recitals made in the documents.

10.15 The assessee has cited decisions of various Hon'ble Courts in paras 5.14 to 5.20 of objections, which are discussed as under :-

S. No.	Decision cited by the assessee	Actual facts of the cited decisions and how these facts are different from the facts in the case of the assessee M/s. RRPR Holding P. Ltd.
1	CIT vs Batra Bhatta Company 321 ITR 526 (Del)	In the cited case, the AO had recorded in reasons that the claim of the assessee that the land is agricultural and hence not a capital asset 'requires much deeper scrutiny'. There was no indication as to on what information or on what material the Assessing Officer harboured the belief that the claim of the assessee required deeper scrutiny. Further, the CIT(A) had also recorded a finding of fact in his order that there was no new material on record.
		In the present case, the material has been specified by the AO in the reasons and the AO has elaborated the facts in detail as to how the income has escaped assessment.
2	ITO vs Lakhmani Mewal Das 103 ITR 437 (SC)	The cited case pertains to the period before amendment in section 147 and true and full disclosure was one of the conditions for reopening in the cited case.
		In the present case, the reopening is within 4 years and hence, first proviso to section 147 regarding full and true disclosure is not applicable.
3	CIT vs Kelvinator of India Ltd. 320 ITR 561 (SC)	In the cited case, the Hon'ble Supreme Court has observed that there should be fresh material for reopening, because change of opinion is a built in concept in section 147 even after amendment.
		The cited case actually helps the cause of Revenue, because in the present case, there is fresh material recorded by the AO in the reasons itself. Further, when even the basic details, i.e. the loan agreement with

		VCPL, were not furnished during the assessment proceedings, then there cannot be a case of change of opinion.
4	*Asoke Kumar Sen vs ITO 132 ITR 707 (Del)*	In the cited case, the ITO sought to justify 'reasons to believe' on the basis of mere affidavit that he entertained such belief. The Hon'ble High Court held that there was nothing in the affidavit to suggest that the ITO had any material before him that would warrant a belief that a part of the income of the petitioner had escaped assessment by reason of his failure to make a true and full disclosure of the material facts. In the present case, there is fresh material referred to in the reasons and the condition regarding full and true disclosure is not applicable.
5	*CIT vs Daulat Ram Rawatmull 87 ITR 349 (SC)*	In the cited case, the Hon'ble Supreme Court had observed in the context of section 69B that there should be a direct nexus between facts and conclusion. In the instant case, the facts recorded in reasons amply corroborate the conclusion of escapement of income.
6	*Sheo Nath Singh vs AAC 82 ITR 147 (SC)*	In the cited case, the Hon'ble Supreme Court has observed that belief must be that of an honest and reasonable person based upon reasonable grounds and that the ITO may act on direct or circumstantial evidence but not on mere suspicion, gossip or rumour. The cited case actually helps the Revenue, because in the present case, the material forming reason to believe is duly recorded in the reasons.
7	*United Electrical Co. P. Ltd. Vs CIT 258 ITR 317 (Del)*	In the cited case, the belief was formed on the basis of a confession in the statement of one Mr. V.K. Jain, which was not actually found in the said statement. There are no such facts in the present case.
8	*Bawa Abhai Singh 253 ITR 83 (Del)*	Discussed separately in para 10.16 below.
9	*Indian Oil Corporation vs ITO 159 ITR 956 (SC)*	In the cited case, the Hon'ble Supreme Court had observed in the context of 'full and true disclosure' that *"11 ... It must further be reiterated that before an action is taken under clause (a) of section 147, there must be reason to believe that there was failure or omission on the part of the assessee to disclose fully and truly all primary facts—See in this connection the observations of this Court in the case of Sheo Nath Singh v. AAC [1971] 82 ITR 147 at p. 153. But reason to believe is not the same thing as reason to suspect."* In the present case, firstly, the condition regarding full and true disclosure is not applicable and secondly, the material has been specified by the AO in the reasons and the AO has elaborated the facts in detail as to how the income has escaped assessment.

10.16 Regarding the cited decision of Hon'ble Delhi High Court in the case of Bawa Abhai Singh 253 ITR 83 (Del), it is observed that the decision is actually in favour of the Revenue and in the cited case, the Hon'ble High Court has observed as under :-

"11. ... that information must be something more than rumour or gossip or hunch. There must be some material which can be regarded as information, on the basis of which the Assessing Officer can have reason to believe that action under section 147 is called for. Jurisdiction of the Court to interfere is very limited, as the Court does not act as appellate

-Disposal of Objections in the case of M/s. RRPR Holding Private Limited for AY 2010-11-

		VCPL, were not furnished during the assessment proceedings, then there cannot be a case of change of opinion.
4	Asoke Kumar Sen vs ITO 132 ITR 707 (Del)	In the cited case, the ITO sought to justify 'reasons to believe' on the basis of mere affidavit that he entertained such belief. The Hon'ble High Court held that there was nothing in the affidavit to suggest that the ITO had any material before him that would warrant a belief that a part of the income of the petitioner had escaped assessment by reason of his failure to make a true and full disclosure of the material facts. In the present case, there is fresh material referred to in the reasons and the condition regarding full and true disclosure is not applicable.
5	CIT vs Daulat Ram Rawatmull 87 ITR 349 (SC)	In the cited case, the Hon'ble Supreme Court had observed in the context of section 69B that there should be a direct nexus between facts and conclusion. In the instant case, the facts recorded in reasons amply corroborate the conclusion of escapement of income.
6	Sheo Nath Singh vs AAC 82 ITR 147 (SC)	In the cited case, the Hon'ble Supreme Court has observed that belief must be that of an honest and reasonable person based upon reasonable grounds and that the ITO may act on direct or circumstantial evidence but not on mere suspicion, gossip or rumour. The cited case actually helps the Revenue, because in the present case, the material forming reason to believe is duly recorded in the reasons.
7	United Electrical Co. P. Ltd. Vs CIT 258 ITR 317 (Del)	In the cited case, the belief was formed on the basis of a confession in the statement of one Mr. V.K. Jain, which was not actually found in the said statement. There are no such facts in the present case.
8	Bawa Abhai Singh 253 ITR 83 (Del)	Discussed separately in para 10.16 below.
9	Indian Oil Corporation vs ITO 159 ITR 956 (SC)	In the cited case, the Hon'ble Supreme Court had observed in the context of 'full and true disclosure' that "11. ... It must further be reiterated that before an action is taken under clause (a) of section 147, there must be reason to believe that there was failure or omission on the part of the assessee to disclose fully and truly all primary facts—See in this connection the observations of this Court in the case of Sheo Nath Singh v. AAC [1971] 82 ITR 147 at p. 153. But reason to believe is not the same thing as reason to suspect." In the present case, firstly, the condition regarding full and true disclosure is not applicable and secondly, the material has been specified by the AO in the reasons and the AO has elaborated the facts in detail as to how the income has escaped assessment.

10.16 Regarding the cited decision of Hon'ble Delhi High Court in the case of Bawa Abhai Singh 253 ITR 83 (Del), it is observed that the decision is actually in favour of the Revenue and in the cited case, the Hon'ble High Court has observed as under :-

"11. ... that information must be something more than rumour or gossip or hunch. There must be some material which can be regarded as information, on the basis of which the Assessing Officer can have reason to believe that action under section 147 is called for. Jurisdiction of the Court to interfere is very limited, as the Court does not act as appellate

-Disposal of Objections in the case of M/s. RRPR Holding Private Limited for AY 2010-11-

authority. No meticulous examination of the information by the Court is permissible to decide for itself as to whether action under section 147 is called for. The 'reason to believe' must be tenable in law. Only if the information or the reason has no nexus with the belief or there is no material or tangible information for forming of requisite belief, then only the Court can interfere, otherwise not.

12. Information means the communication or reception of knowledge or intelligence. It includes knowledge obtained from investigation, study or insurrection. To inform means to impart knowledge. A detail available in the papers filed before the ITO does not by its mere presence or availability become an item of information. It is transmuted into an item of information only if and when its existence is realised and its implications are recognised. Whether a particular fact or material constitutes information in a particular case has to be decided with reference to the facts of that case and there cannot be a definite rule of universal application as to when a particular material will be taken to be an information."

(Emphasis supplied)

10.17 The above is without prejudice to the fact that the condition regarding full and true disclosure, which is contained in the 1st Proviso to section 147, applies only to case in which the assessment is sought to be reopened after 4 years from the end of the relevant assessment year. In the assessee's case, the reopening is made within 4 years and hence, the 1st Proviso to section 147 is not applicable in this case.

10.18 In the case of the present assessee, the reasons for forming the belief are discussed in detail in the reasons and the material forming the basis of such belief is also duly referred to in the reasons. This material is the tax evasion petitions received against the assessee, the information and details filed by the assessee in the proceedings for the subsequent year, report dated 10.05.2015 received from the office of DGIT (Investigation), etc. The reasons to believe have direct nexus with the material so received. Hence, the cited decision of Hon'ble Delhi High Court in the case of Bawa Abhai Singh 253 ITR 83 (Del) helps the cause of Revenue and reliance is placed on the same.

10.19 In view of the above discussion, the assessee's contention that reasons recorded are based on no material to initiate action u/s 147 of the Act is incorrect and hence rejected.

11. **That reasons recorded are in any case not based on any fresh tangible material which surfaced after furnishing of return of income and as such, initiation of proceedings u/s 147 of the Act is without jurisdiction**

11.1 The assessee has contended that there is no fresh material, which surfaced after completion of assessment and till the date of initiation of reassessment proceedings. The assessee has cited decisions of various Hon'ble Courts in support of its contention on this issue.

11.2 On this issue, it is observed that the assessee's contention is incorrect on facts. The fresh material forming basis of reopening has been duly referred to by the AO while recording reasons. All this material is received after 30.03.2013, i.e. the date of completion of regular assessment u/s 143(3) of the Act as detailed in the following paragraph.

11.3 Subsequent to the completion of assessment for AY 2010-11 on 30.03.2013, fresh information surfaced from the following three sources :-

Source 1   Tax Evasion Petitions ("TEPs") received from a shareholder of NDTV from 29.06.2013 onwards.

Source 2   Copy of loan agreement regarding receipt of interest free loan of Rs. 403.85 crore by the assessee titled as "Loan Agreement dated 21.07.2009 between VCPL and RRPR and Prannoy Roy and Radhika Roy" was furnished by the assessee

Page 15 of 18

157

NDTV FRAUDS

company for the first time along with its reply dated 10.02.2015 filed during the course of assessment proceedings for AY 2012-13.

Source 3   The article dated 14.01.2015 published on the website www.newslaundry.com, which corroborated the facts and the dubious nature of transaction of receipt of interest free loan of Rs. 403.85 crore by the assessee.

11.4   Since crucial and sufficient fresh material surfaced after completion of assessment and till the date of initiation of reassessment proceedings, therefore, the assessee's contention on this issue is factually incorrect and the decisions of various Hon'ble Courts cited by the assessee also do not help it. The contention on this issue is hence rejected.

12.   **That no income has escaped assessment and therefore mandatory precondition for invoking of provision u/s 147 is not satisfied**

12.1   The assessee has stated that the AO has not fulfilled the condition regarding escapement of income and therefore, the reopening is invalid. The assessee has cited decisions of various Hon'ble Courts in support of its contention on this issue.

12.2   The assessee's contention is not correct. Perusal of reasons recorded reveals that after recording the facts of the case in the reasons, the AO has given categorical conclusions regarding escapement of income, which are discussed in the following paragraphs.

12.3   In para 11 of the reasons, in the context of interest free loan of Rs. 403.85 crore received by the assessee from VCPL, the AO has observed :-

"Thus, RR and PR no longer have controlling stake in NDTV Limited and apparently no consideration was shown to have received directly in lieu of transfer of their controlling rights in NDTV Limited, by way of transfer of the assessee company."

12.4   In para 12 of the reasons, in the context of purchase of shares of NDTV @ Rs. 4 per share from Dr. Prannoy Roy and Mrs. Radhika Roy when the market rate of shares was Rs. 140 per share, the AO has concluded :-

"In view of the above, it is seen that the assessee company received a direct and tangible benefit arising from the course of its business. The benefit is real one capable of characterized as 'income' and not a notional benefit.

12.5   Further, in para 13 of the reasons, in the context of interest free loan of Rs. 403.85 crore received by the assessee from VCPL, the AO has concluded :-

"13.   It is further noticed that as on August 5,2009, the value of asset/NAV in the books of the assessee was 26% shares of NDTV Ltd only, which would be around Rs. 210 crores. The assessee company however received a consideration of Rs.403.85 crores in the form of 0% convertible unsecured loan and the entire proceeds were used to extinguish a liability of loan and interest to ICICI bank. Thus RRPR immediately benefited by Rs.400 crore i.e 400 crores less Rs.4.62 crores being cost of asset acquired on the same date. This sale consideration has been camouflaged as issue of convertible debenture for avoiding payment of tax on actual transfer of 26% holding in NDTV Limited."

12.6   In the same context, the AO has further observed in para 16 of the reasons recorded as under :-

"16.   As per the report of the DGIT(Investigation) dated 10.05.2011 available on record, it is seen the share capital of VCPL was Rs.1 lac only and it has raised the fund by way of "zero coupon optionally convertible loan" of Rs.403.85 crores from its related company Shinano Retail Private Limited which is a Reliance Group (Mukesh Ambani). The DGIT Investigation has

Page 16 of 18

158

-Disposal of Objections in the case of M/s. RRPR Holding Private Limited for AY 2010-11-

gone into the source of funds of Shinano Retail, which were Reliance Port and Terminal Limited and Reliance Ventures Limited etc, which were found assessed at Mumbai respectively in the report.

As per the new information received, the zero coupon optionally convertible loan given to VCPL was converted into Zero Coupon Optionally Convertible Debenture (OCD) on 30.06.2012 by Shinano Retail. In March 2012, i.e F.Y.11-12, the debenture of Rs.403.85 crores was sold by Shinano to M/s Eminent Network Private Limited for Rs.50 crores. Why Shinano Retail booked the loss on sale of debenture and whether claimed the same as deduction is not known M/s Eminent Network Private Limited is owned by M/s Digivision Cable which is in turn a subsidiary of HFCL as per last information available. Thus it is seen that loan worth Rs.403.85 crores has been acquired by an entity merely for Rs.50 crores. The facts narrated above indicate that the transaction is not a straight forward business transaction, but a convoluted one. The nature and source of transaction is thus not explainable and therefore comes within the ambit of the provisions of section 68 of the Income Tax Act."

12.7   From the above, it can be observed that the AO has not only given conclusive findings regarding escapement of income of the assessee for the year under consideration but has also specified the manner in which such escapement has taken place.

12.8   In view of the above position, the assessee's contention is not acceptable and the same is rejected.

13.   **That proceedings u/s 147 of the Act are proceedings for investigation and, therefore the action is impermissible**

13.1   The assessee has stated that proceedings cannot be initiated for making roving and fishing enquiries. The decisions of various Hon'ble Courts have been cited by the assessee in support of its contention on this issue.

13.2   While the assessee has stated a proposition of law that proceedings for reassessment cannot be initiated for making roving and fishing enquiries, the assessee has not alleged that the reassessment proceedings in its case are initiated for making roving and fishing enquiries and if so how.

13.3   Thus, the proposition advanced by the assessee is not relevant to the present issue. Therefore, the same does not agitate against the reassessment proceedings in the assessee's case.

14.   **That proceedings initiated u/s 147 of the Act are based on change of opinion and therefore, instant proceedings are in excess of jurisdiction**

14.1   The contention is repetitive, because the assessee has already taken up this issue in para 6 of the objections wherein it alleged that no fresh material surfaced after completion of assessment proceedings and till the initiation of reassessment proceedings. The same have already been dealt with in para 14 of the present order, which position is reiterated.

14.2   Since there is fresh material surfaced after the completion of assessment, the benefit of which was not available to the AO during the original assessment proceedings, to the extent that even the basic loan agreement between the assessee and VCPL was not filed during the original assessment proceedings, therefore, there cannot be a case of formation of opinion or change of opinion in the present case.

14.3   The assessee has cited a number of decisions of various Hon'ble Courts to substantiate that the reassessment proceedings shall not be valid in case of change of opinion. However, the cited cases are of no avail to the assessee, because on facts, the present case is not a case of change of opinion and the reopening is based on fresh material which surfaced after completion of original assessment.

Page 17 of 18

NDTV FRAUDS

-Disposal of Objections in the case of M/s. RRPR Holding Private Limited for AY 2010-11-

14.4   Hence, the assessee's contention on this issue is incorrect and is rejected.

15.   As held by various Hon'ble Courts, there has to be prima facie some material on the basis of which the Department could reopen the case. Though the objections have been discussed in detail on the basis of facts also, the sufficiency or final correctness of the material is not a thing to be considered at this stage. And once 'prima facie some material' is present, the Department is not precluded from reopening the assessment. Further, the assessee may present its arguments in detail during the assessment proceedings. And these will be duly considered before completing the assessment.

16.   In view of the above detailed discussion, and after considering the facts of all the cases/judgments cited by the assessee and the submission made by the assessee, the objections raised by the assessee are not found sustainable and the same are hereby rejected and thus stand disposed of. Notice issued u/s 148 of the Income Tax Act, 1961 dated 23.03.2015 is proper and as per law. Therefore, the connected reassessment proceedings u/s 147/148 of the Act, need to be proceeded further. Hence, the reassessment proceedings u/s 147/148 of the Act, are being carried forward as per the provisions of the Income Tax Act, 1961 and Income Tax Rules, 1962.

Sd/-

Dated : 29.01.2016

(Bhupinderjit Kumar)
Dy. Commissioner of Income Tax
Circle-18(1), New Delhi

Copy to the assessee :-

Sd/-

Dy. Commissioner of Income Tax
Circle-18(1), New Delhi

Page 18 of 18

160

43413826R00091

Made in the USA
Middletown, DE
09 May 2017